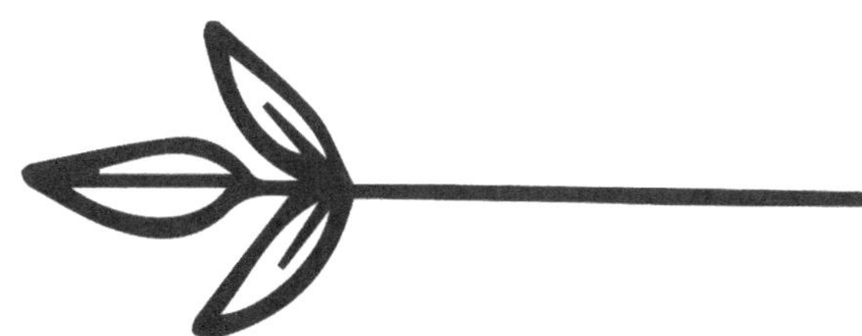

This Book Belongs to:

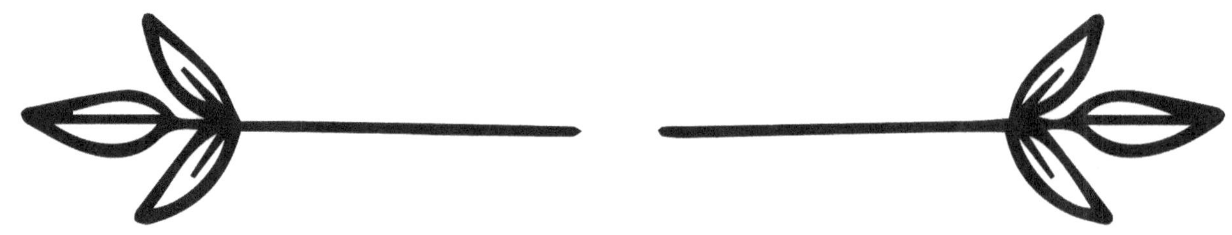

"May this coloring book ignite your imagination and whisk you away to magical lands filled with unicorns, dragons, fairies, and princesses. Let your creativity soar! Happy coloring adventure!"

Leticia Seraphim

Test Color Page

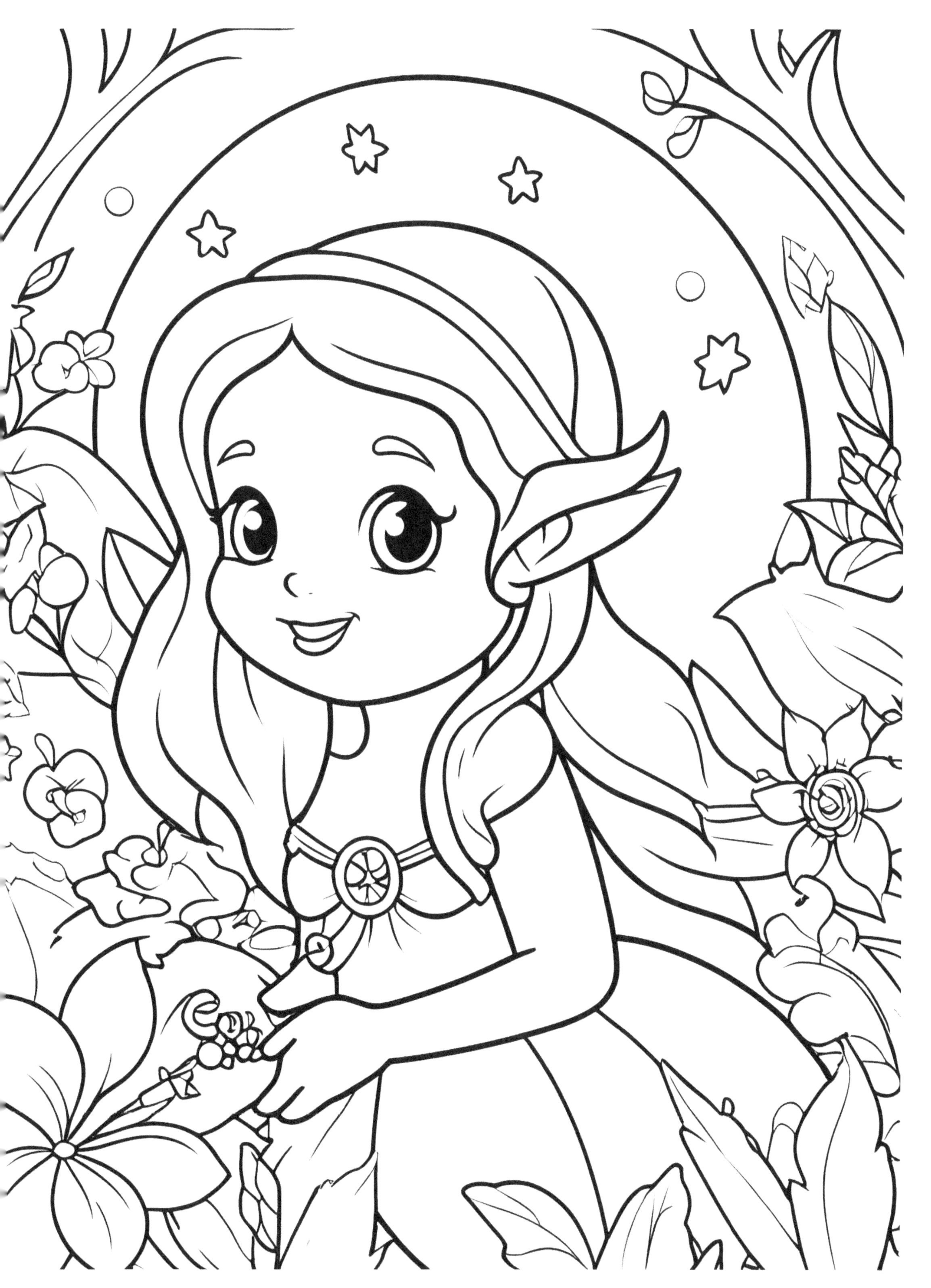

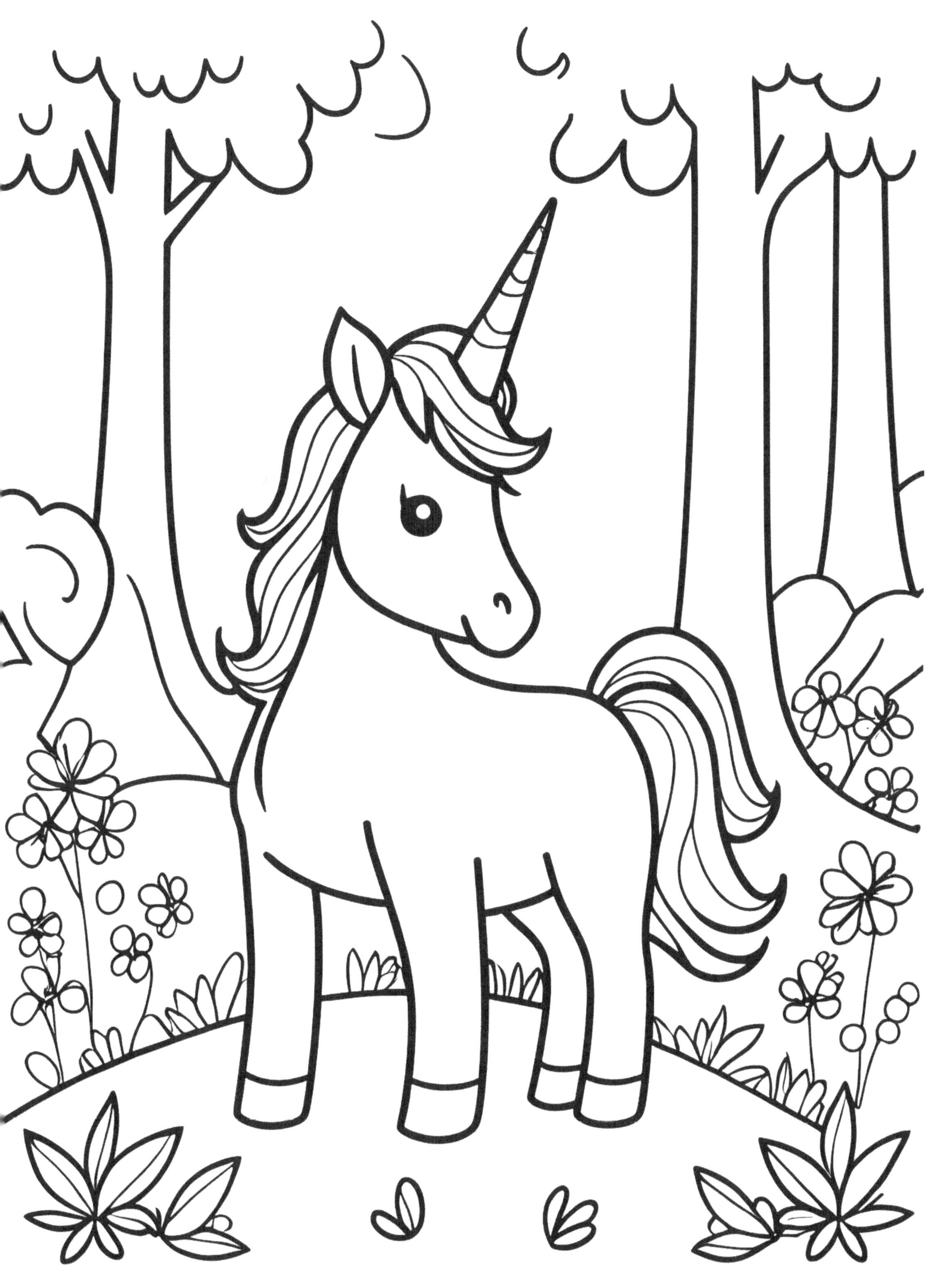

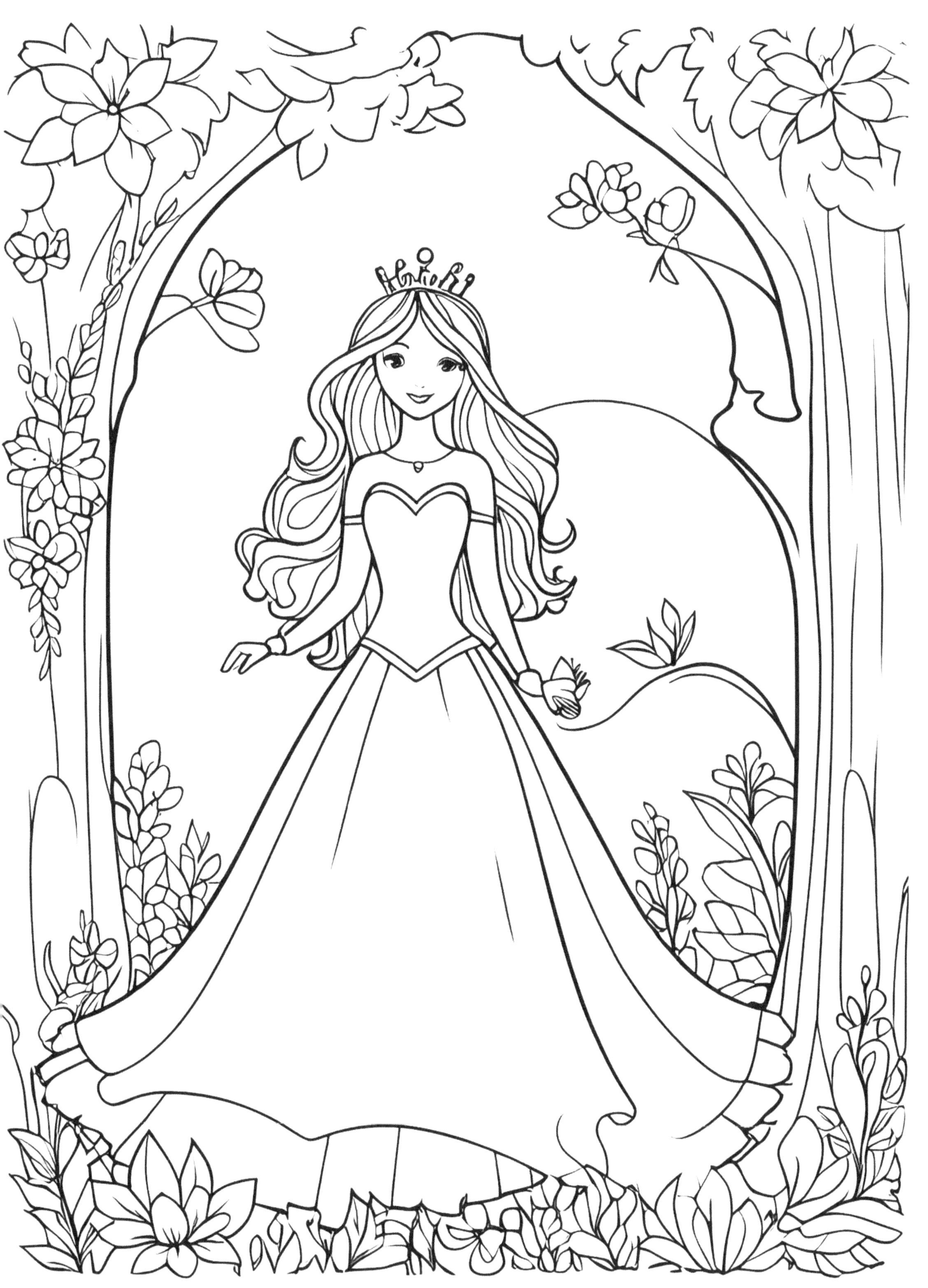

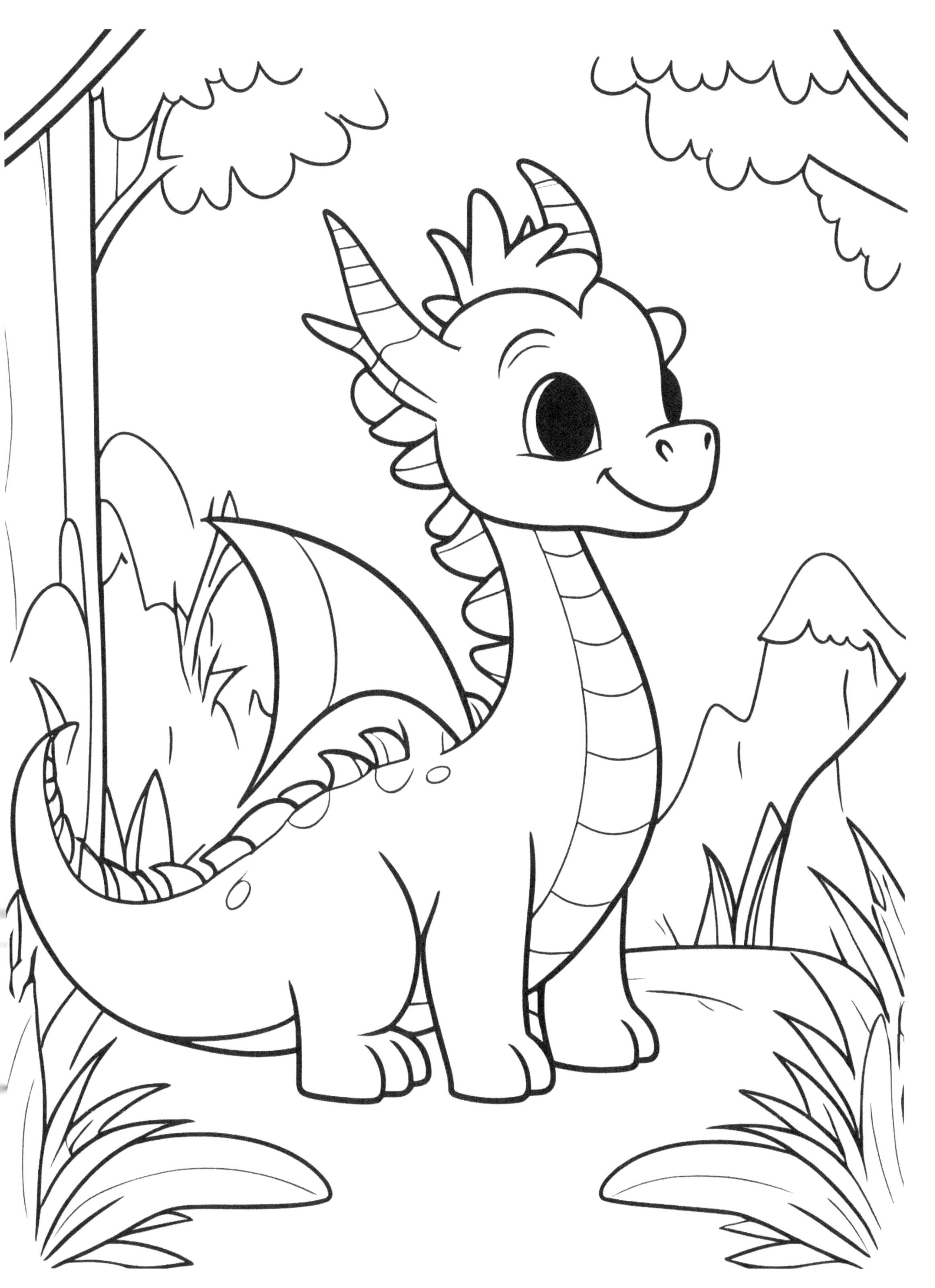

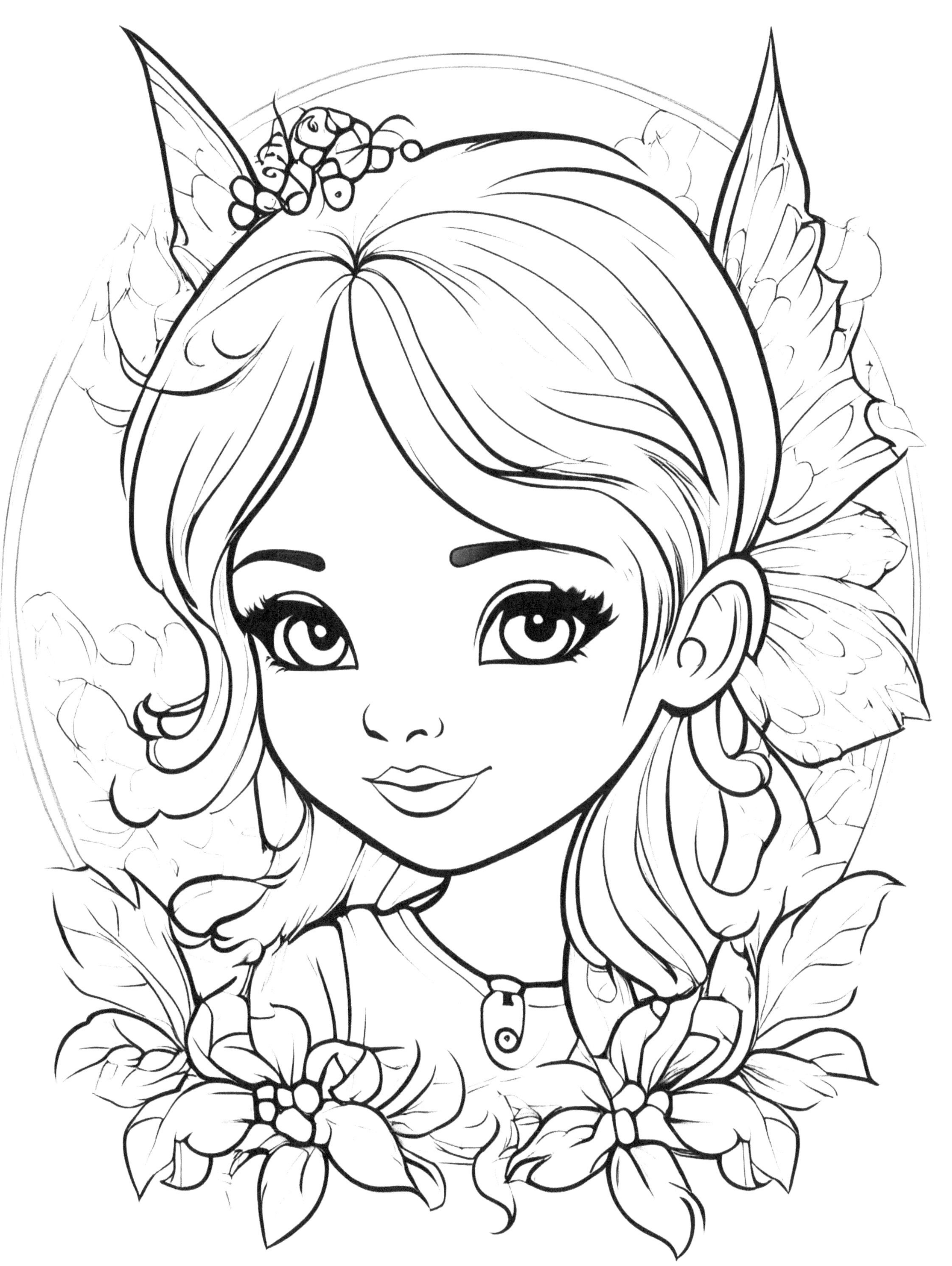

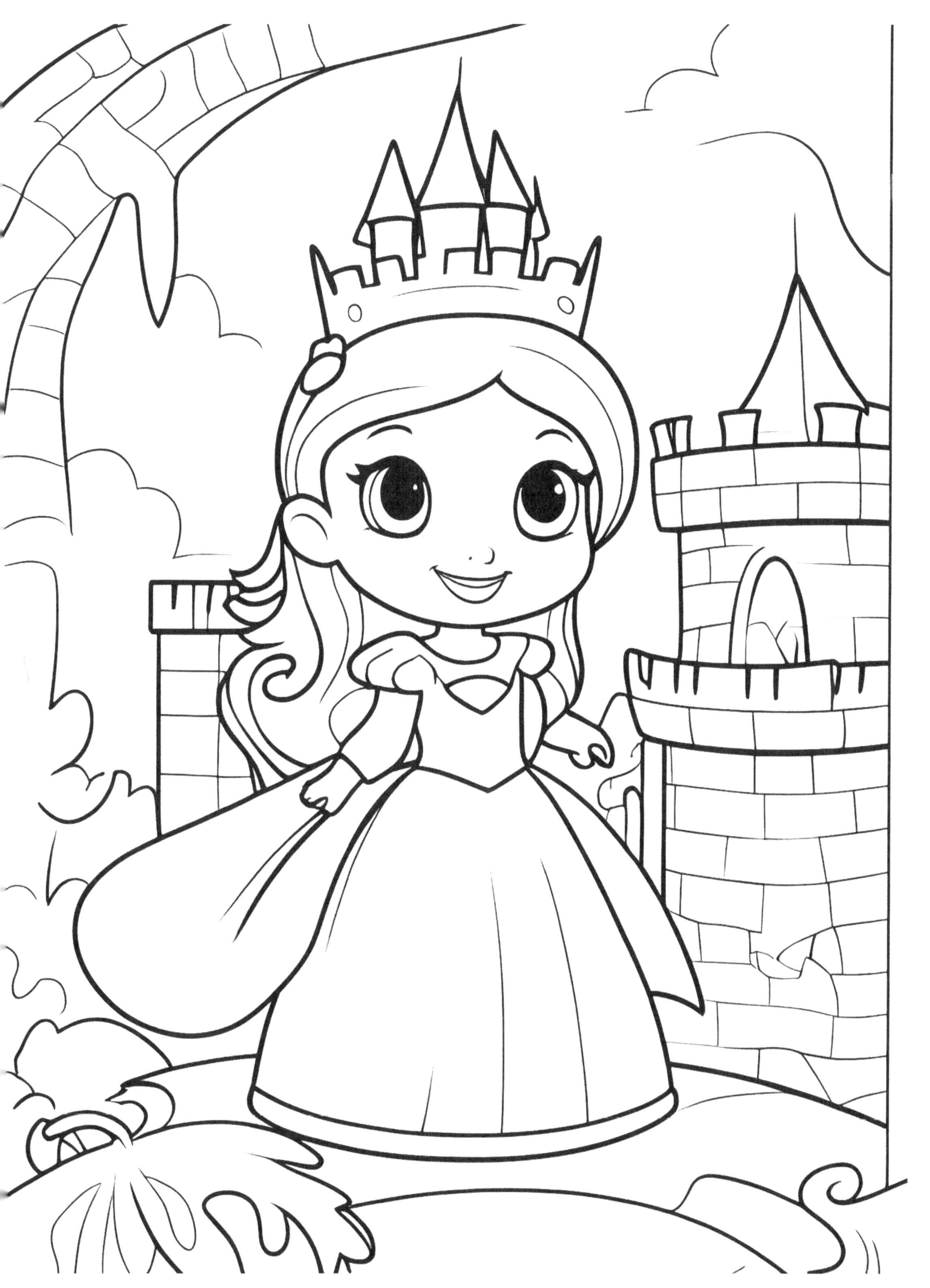

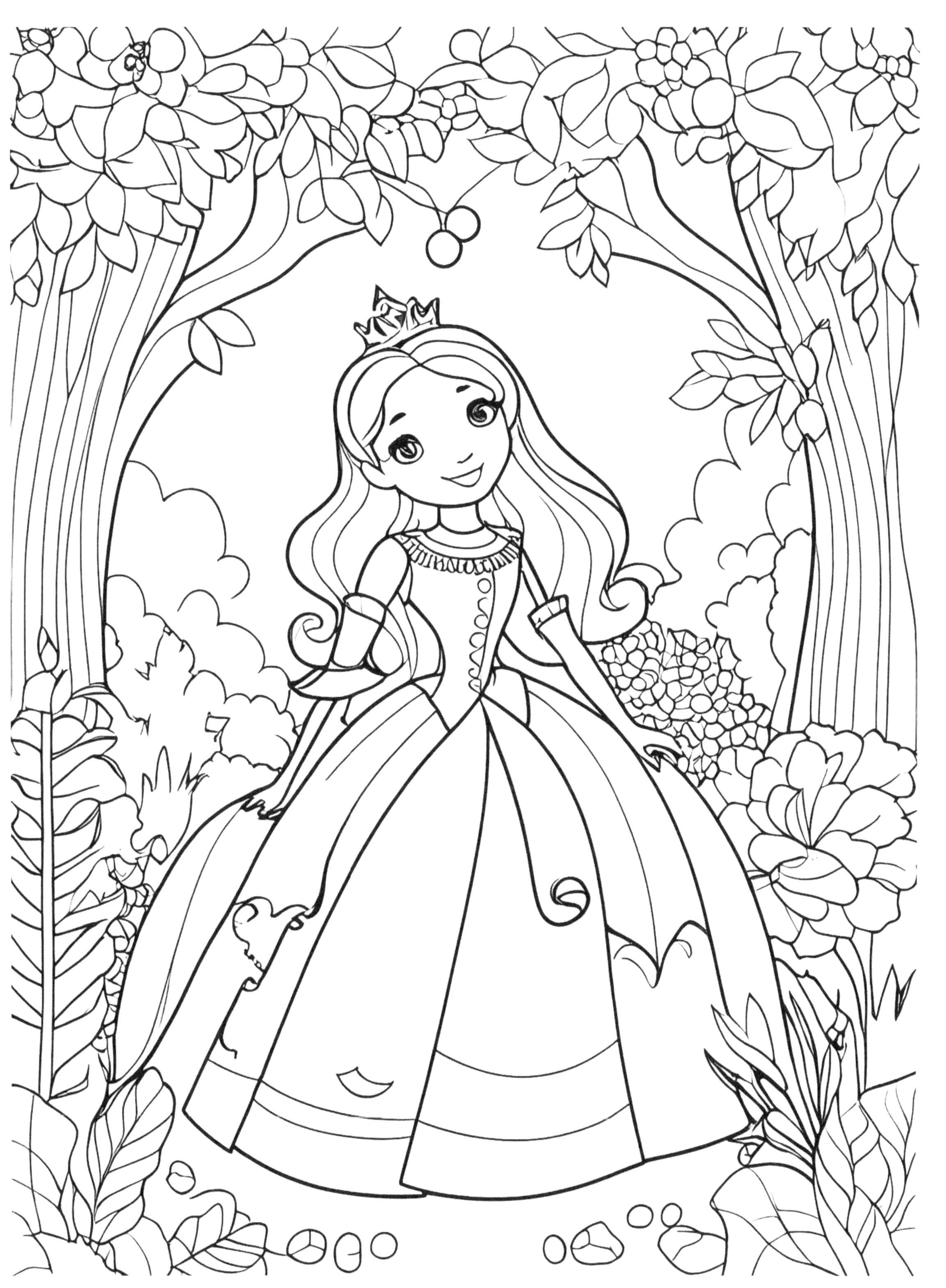

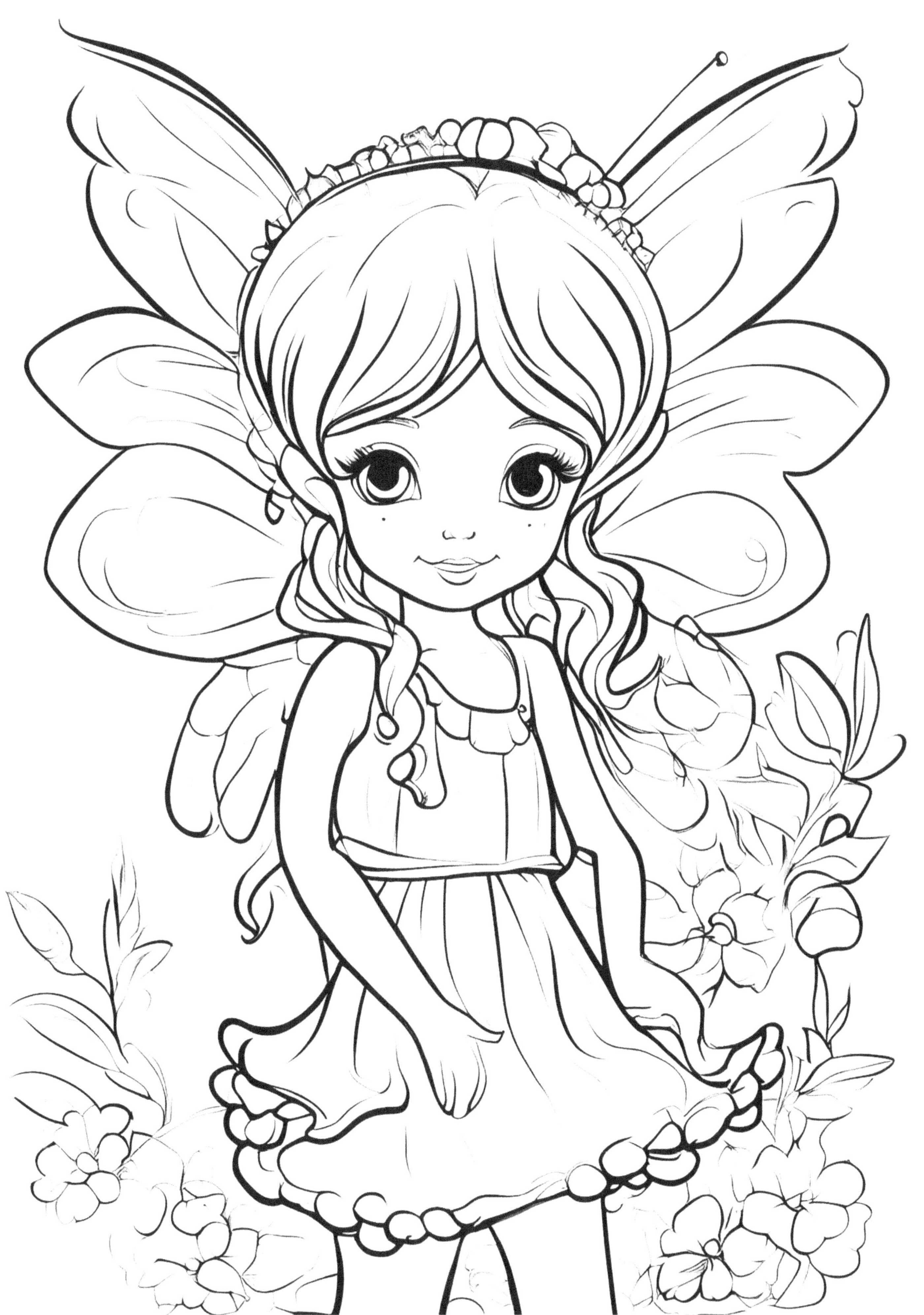

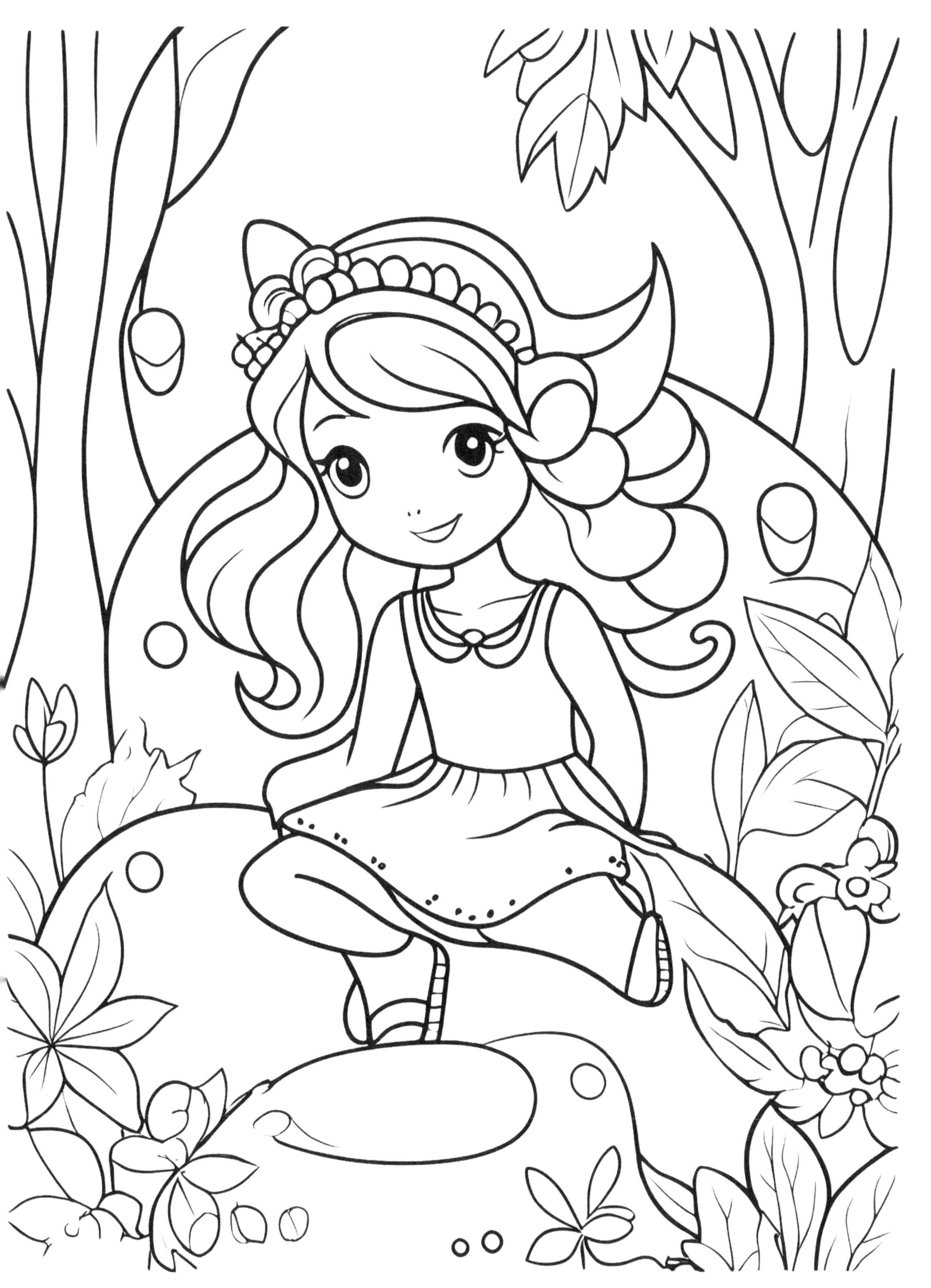

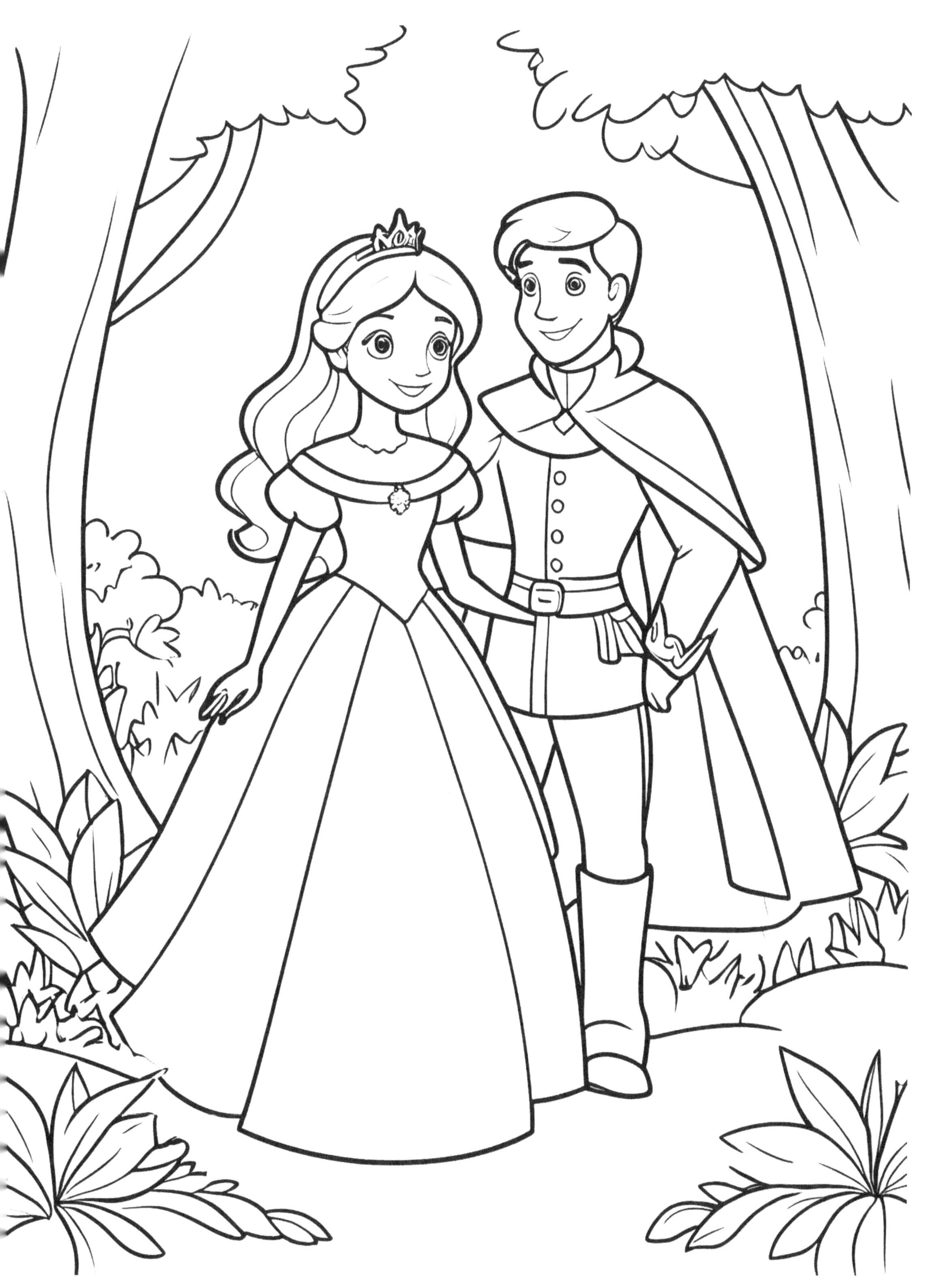

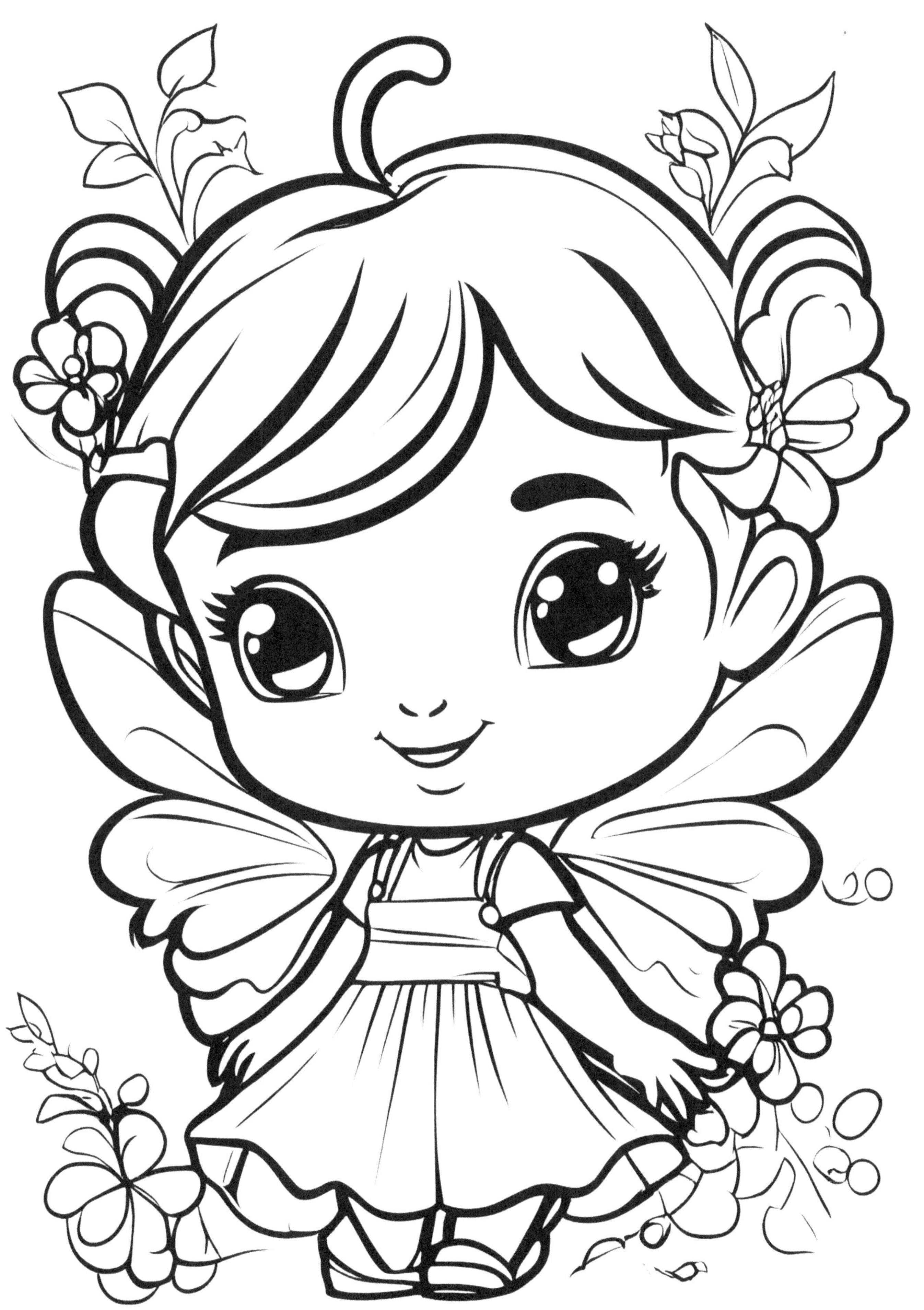

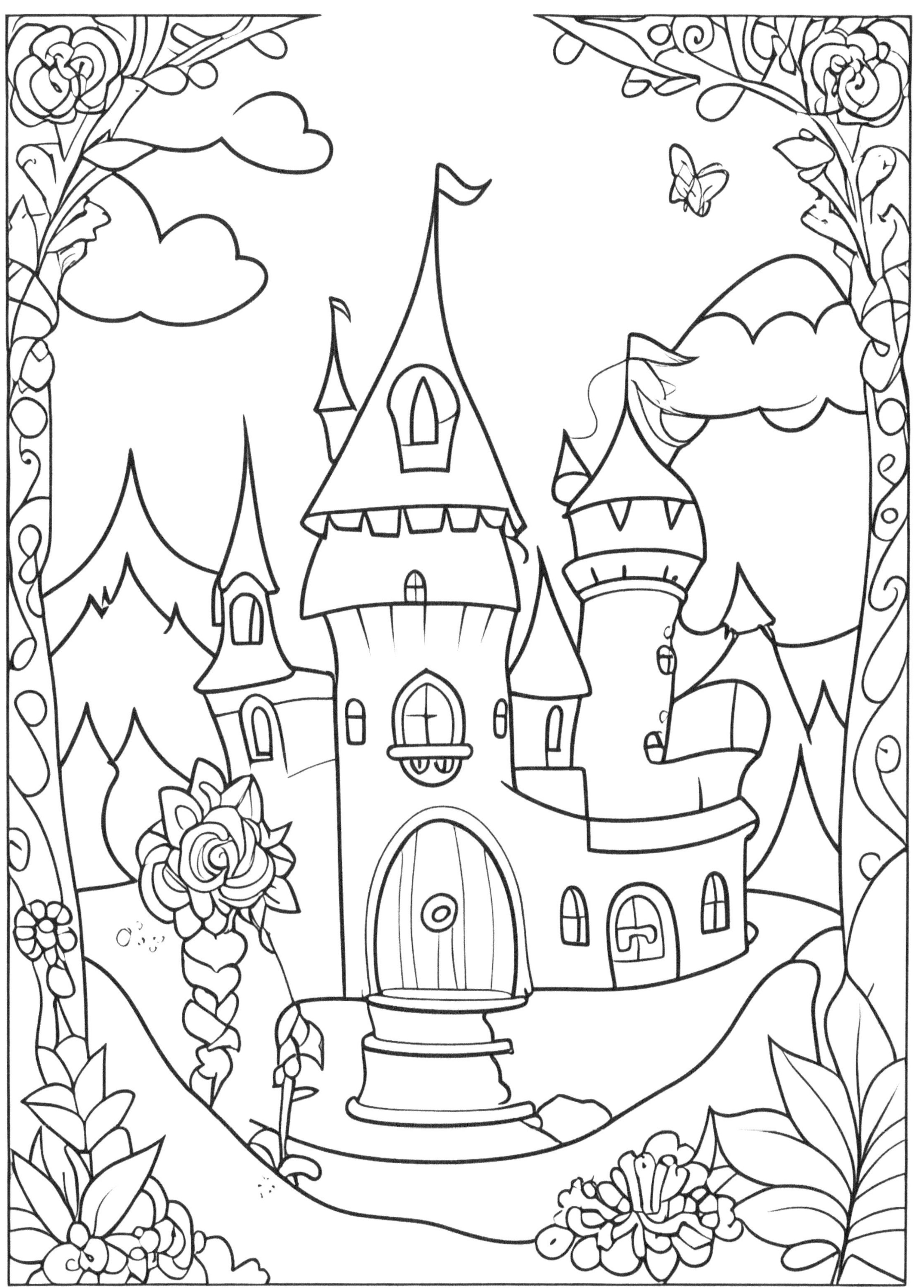

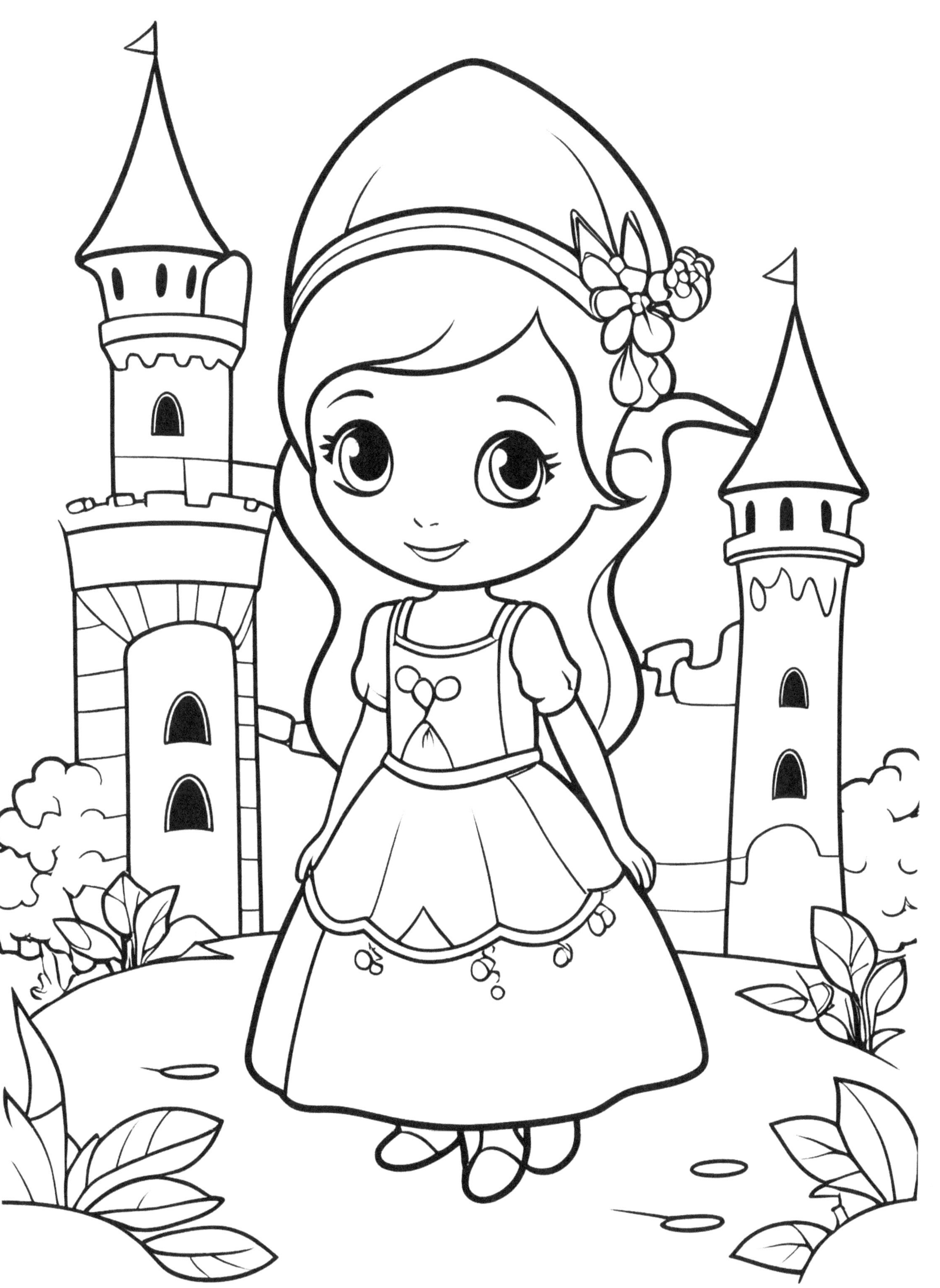

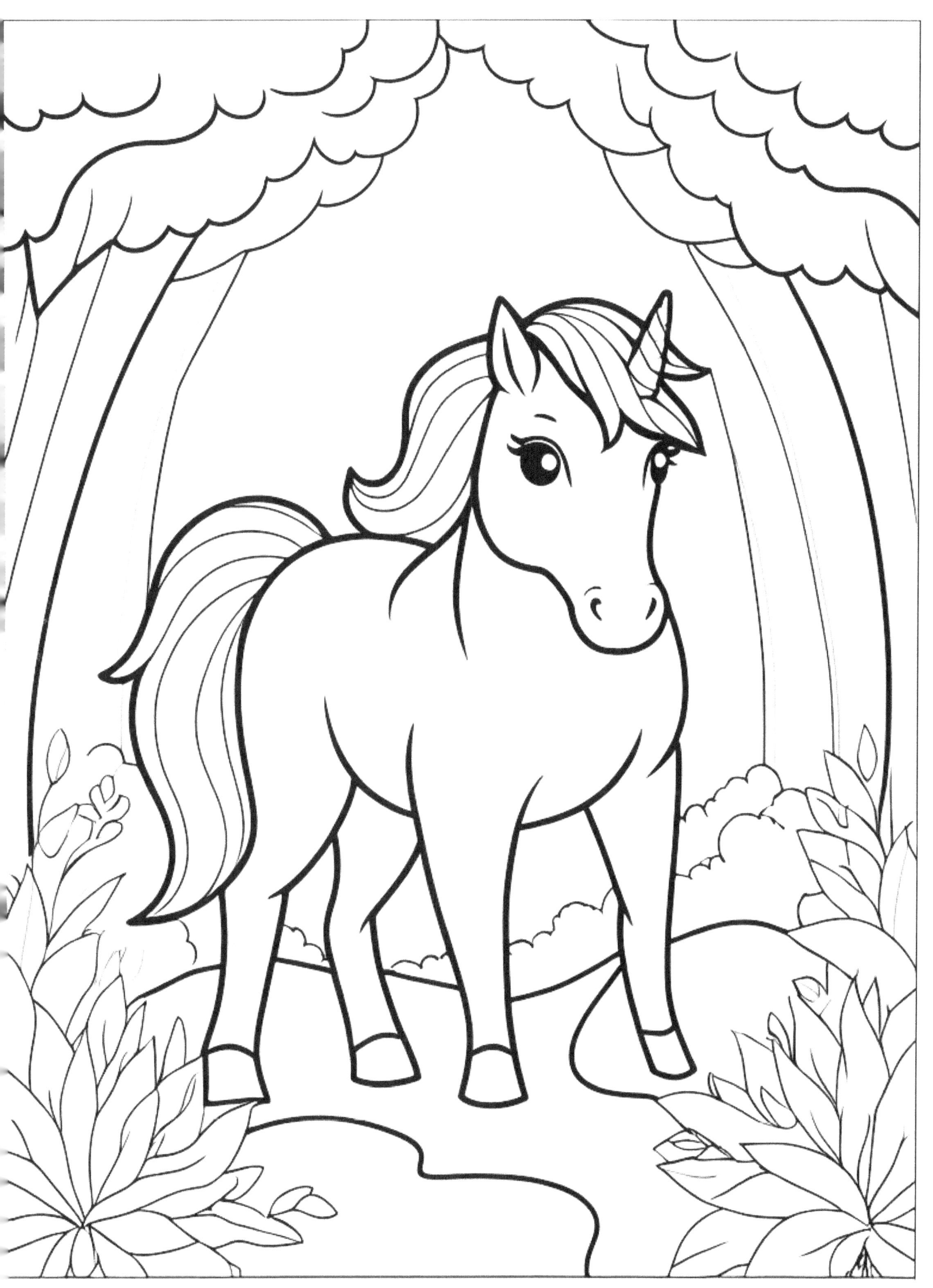

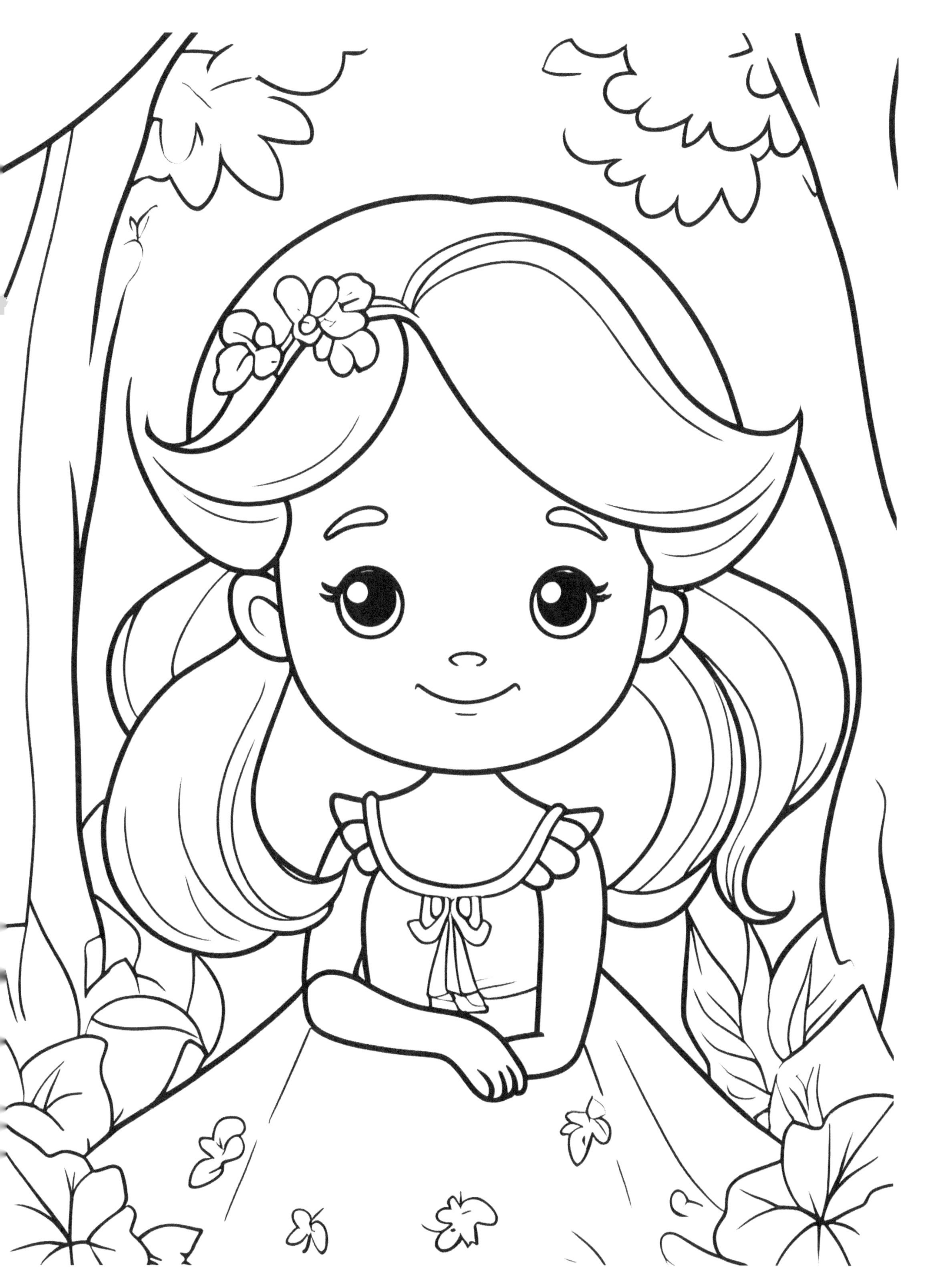

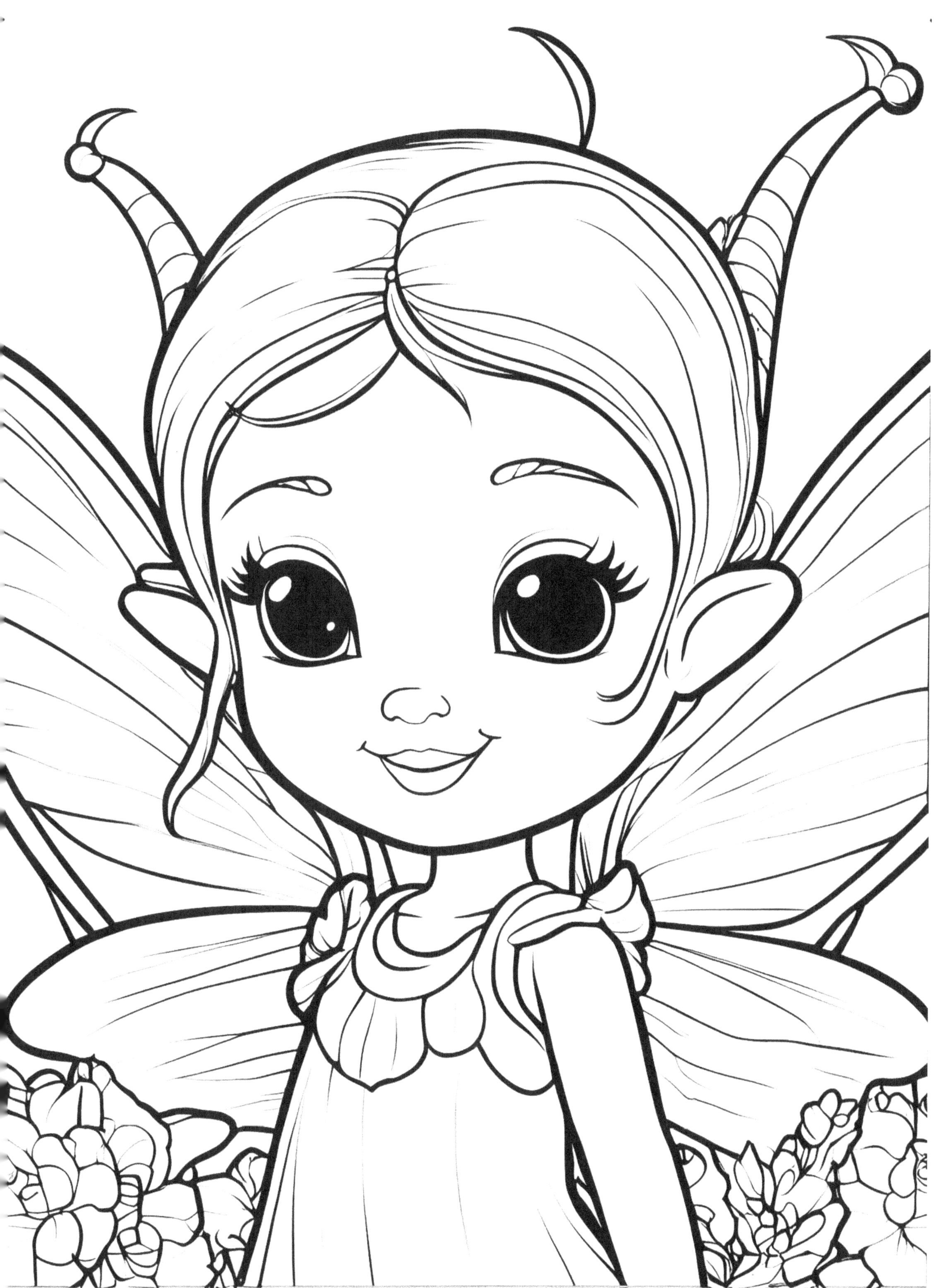

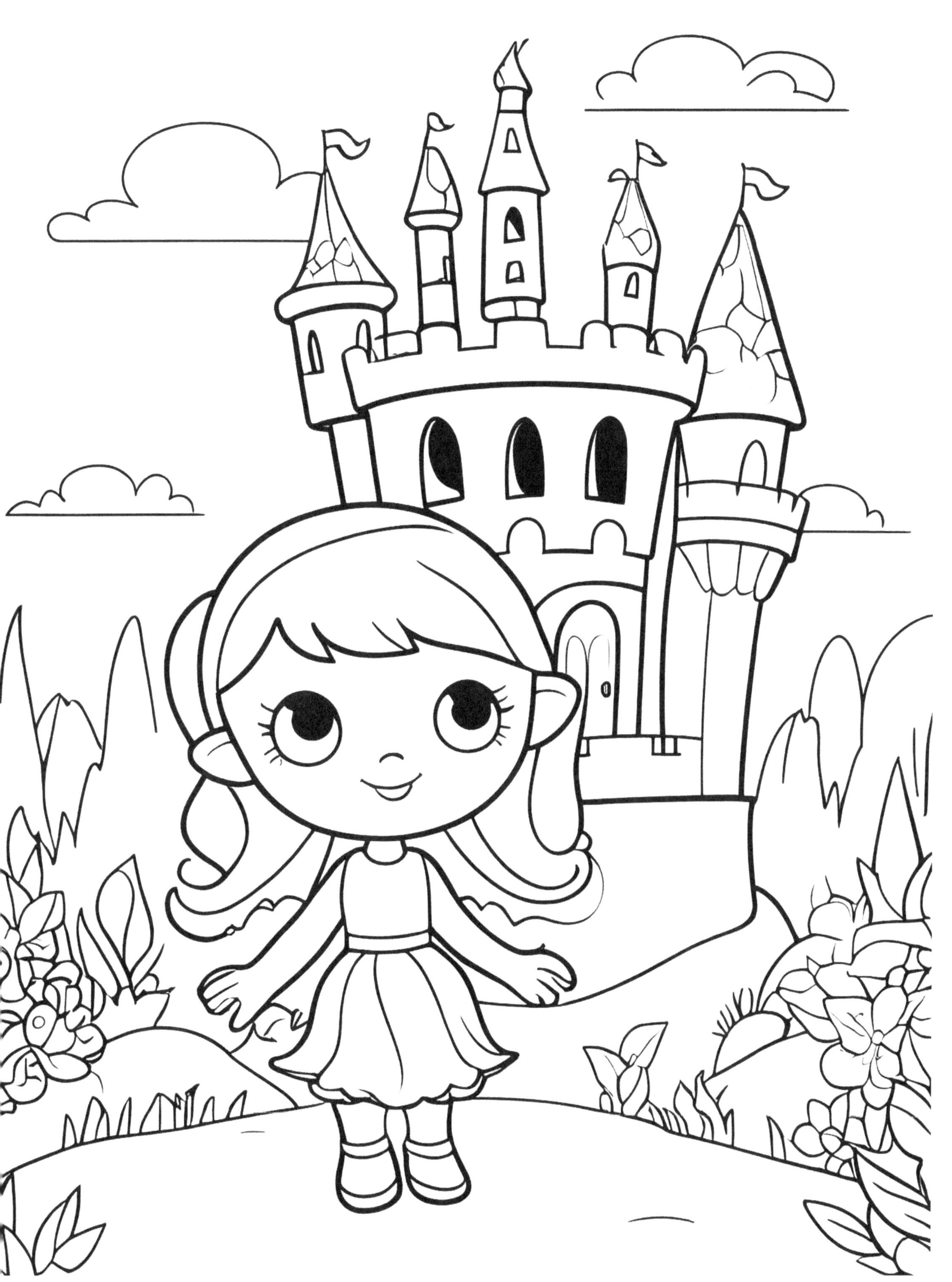

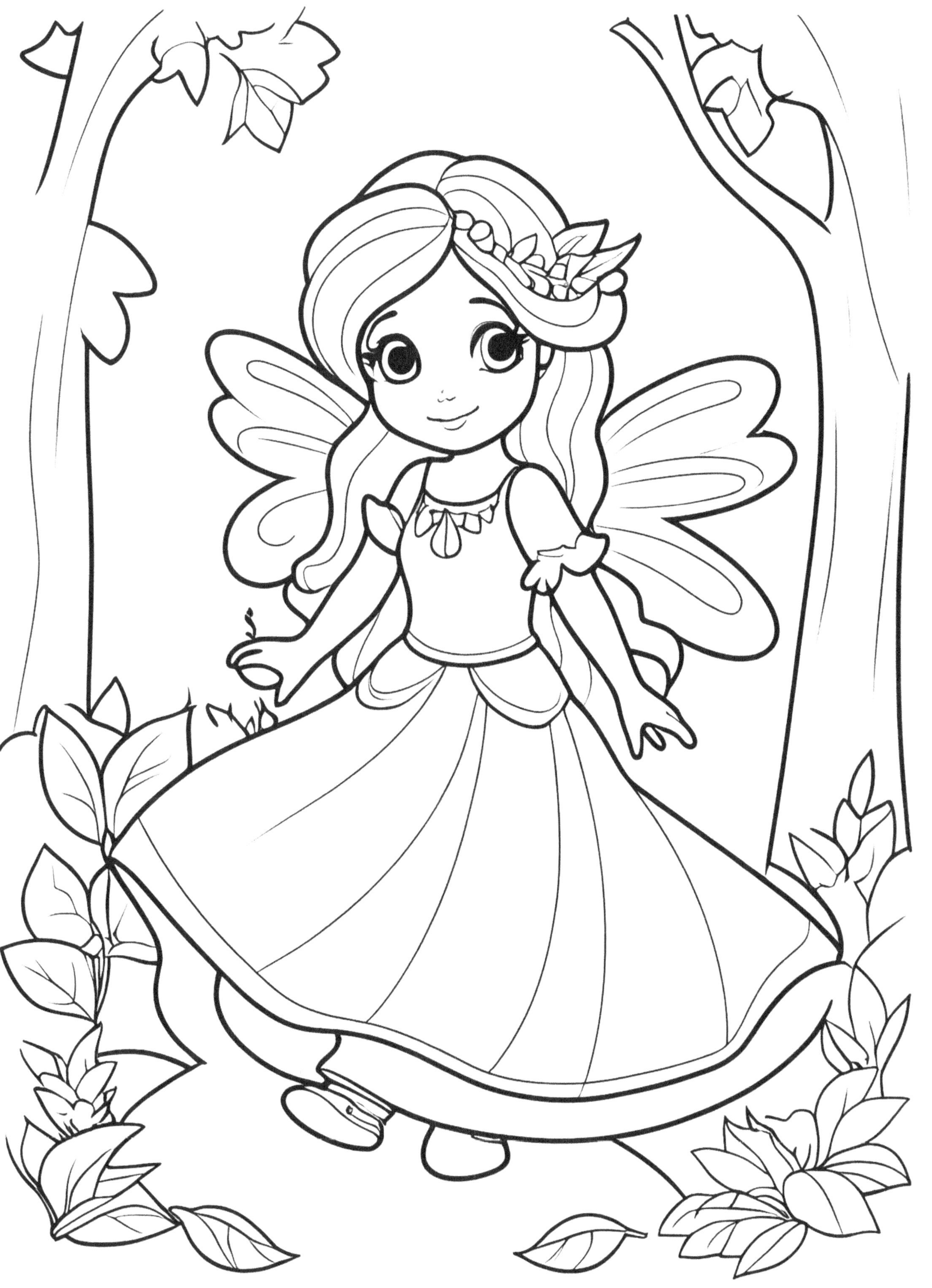

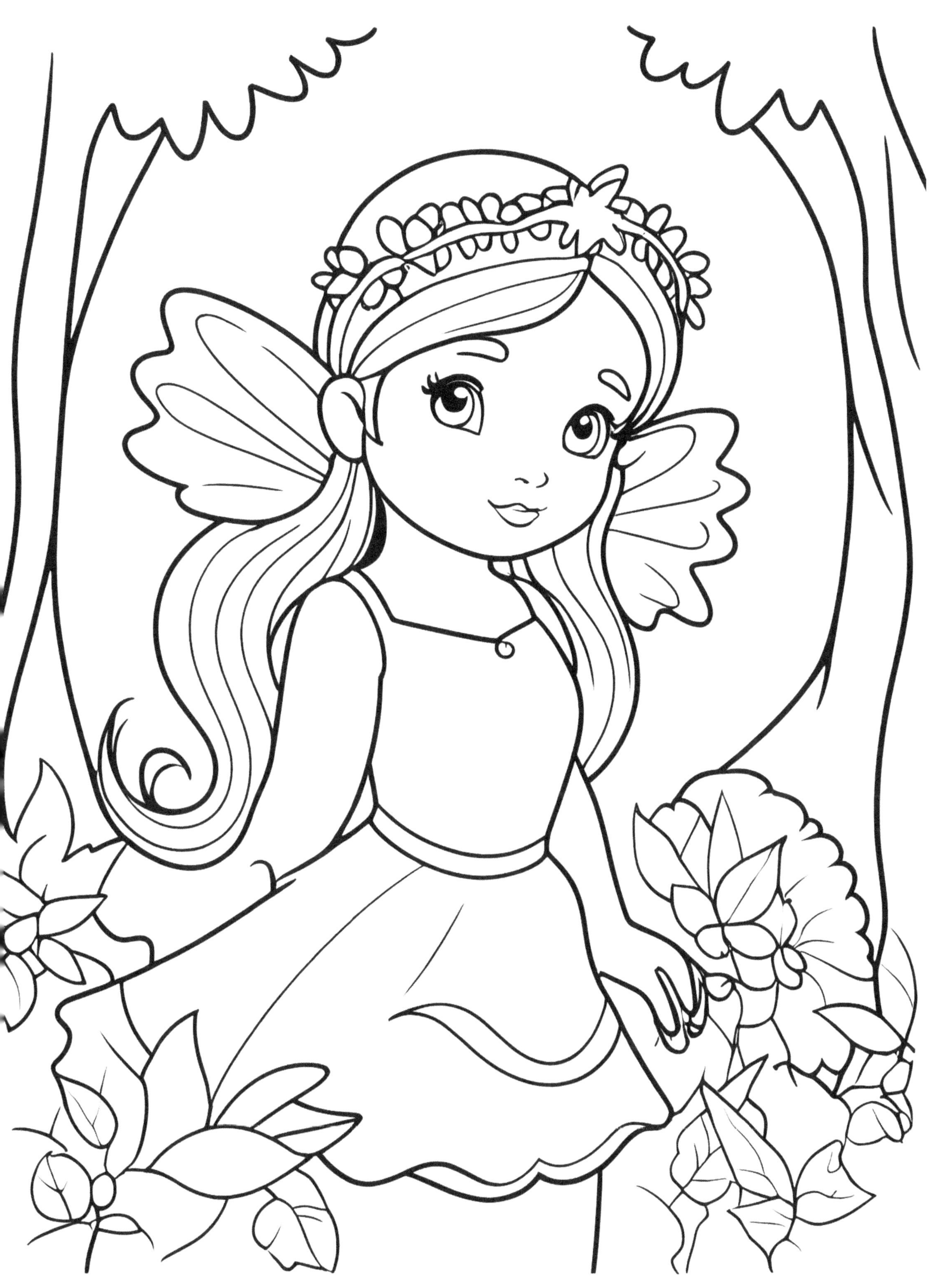

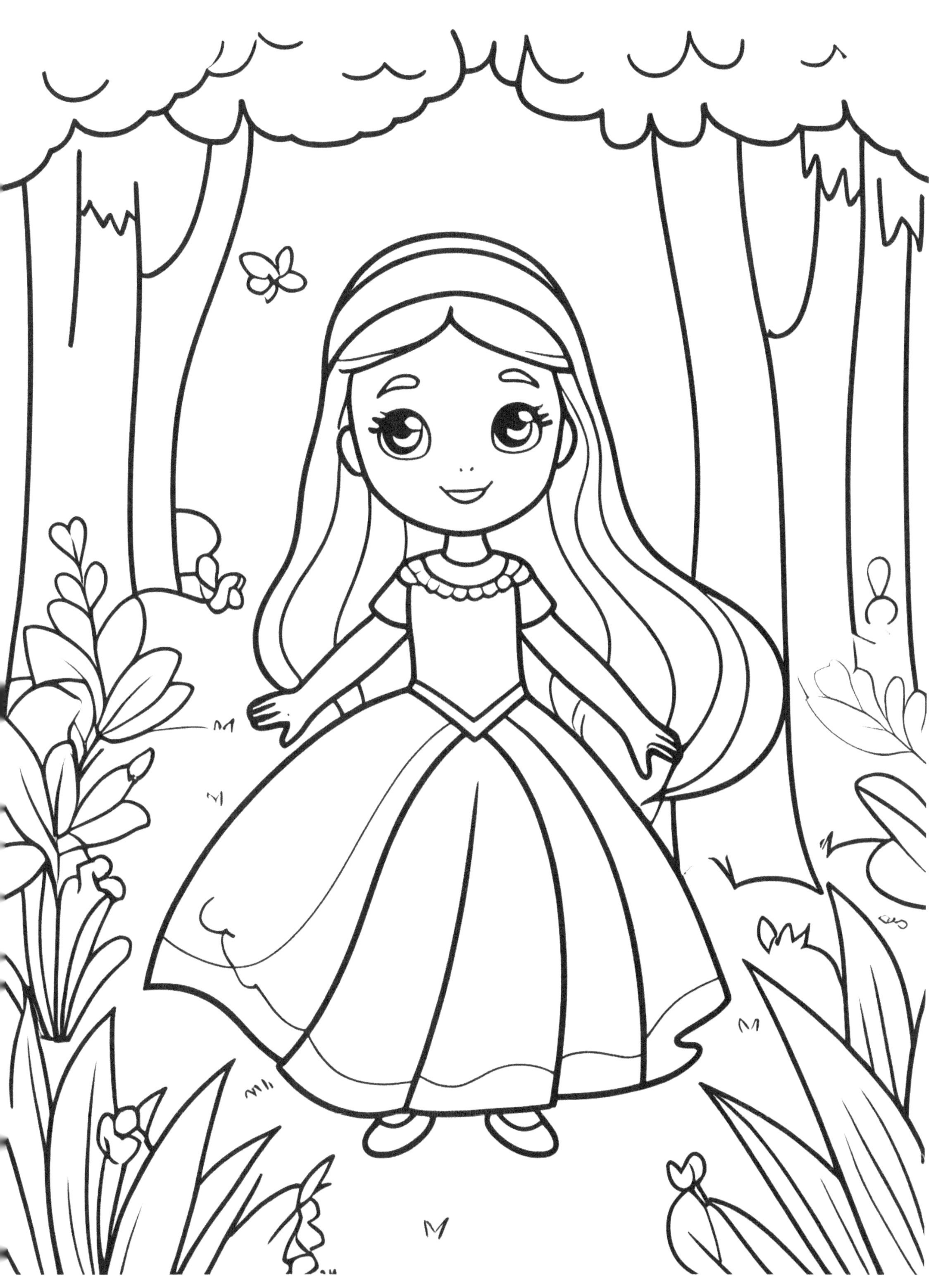

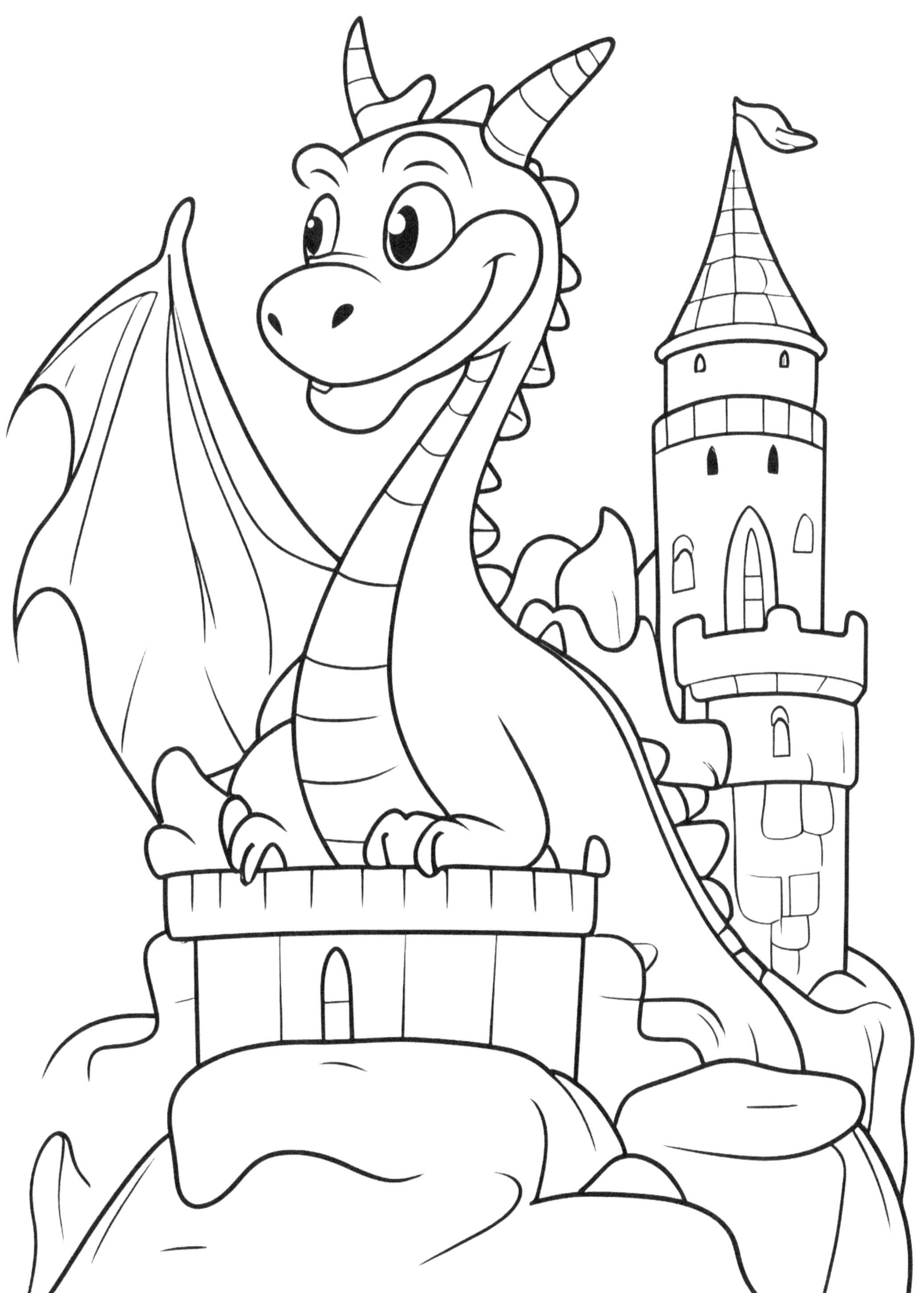

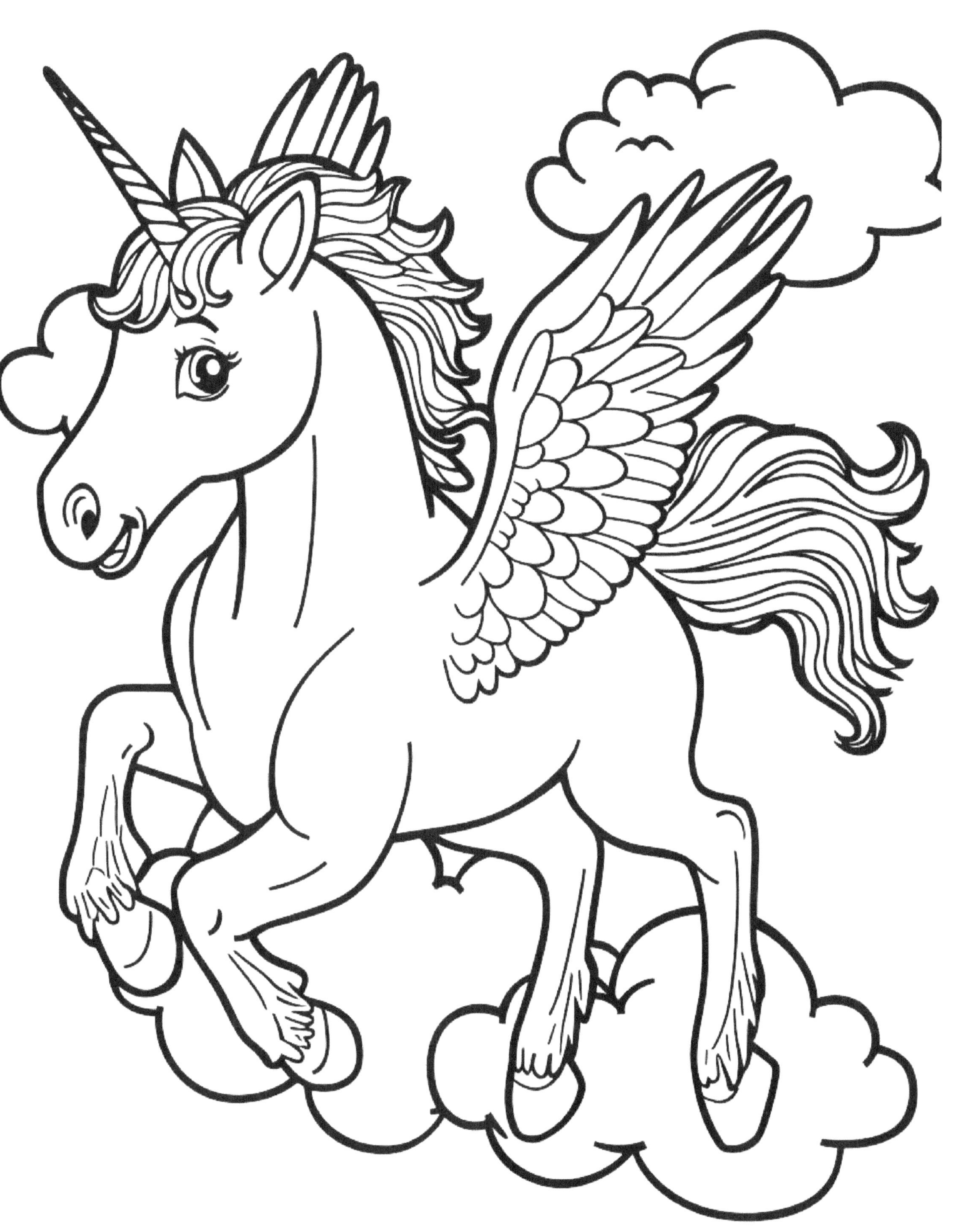

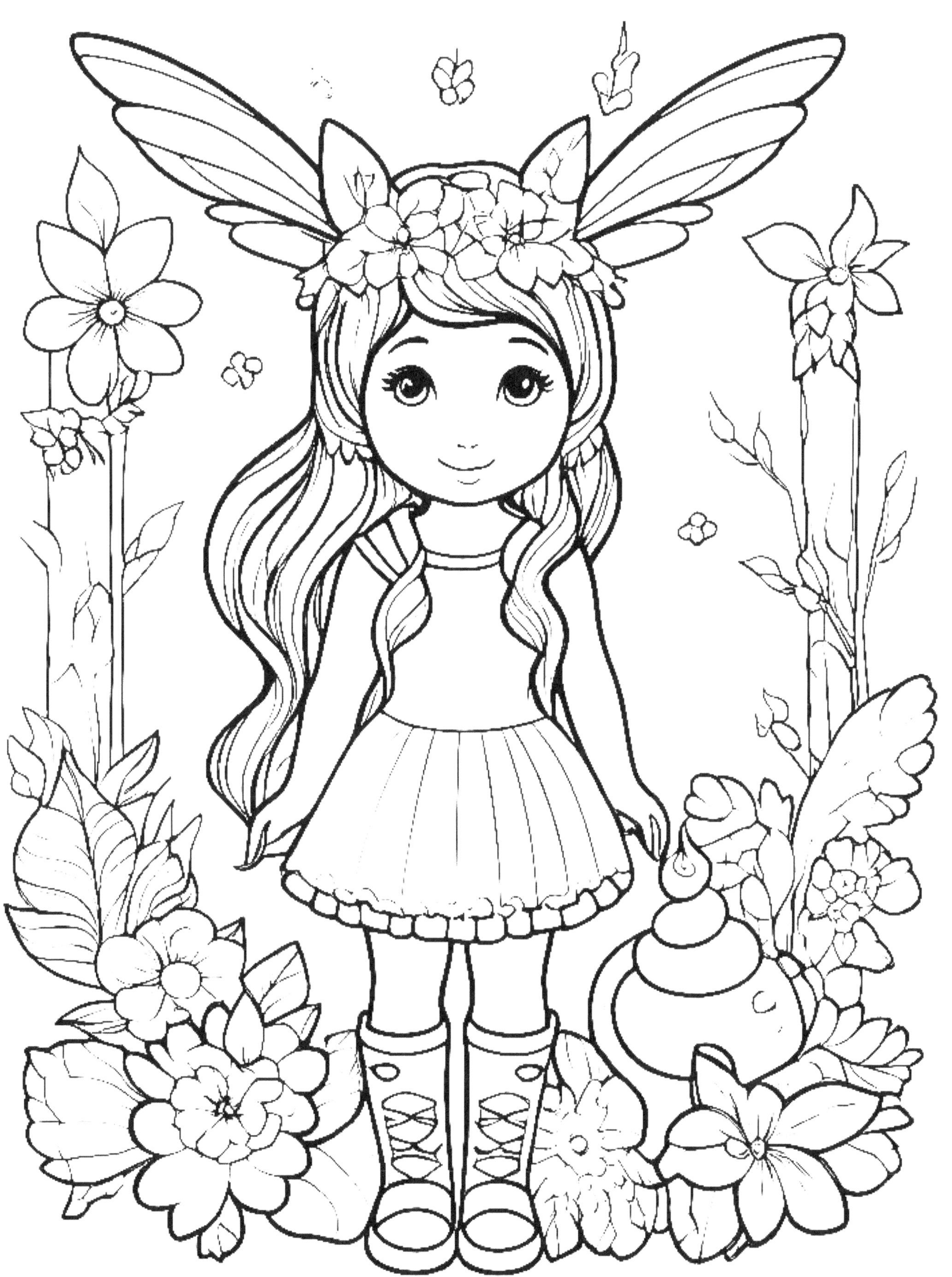

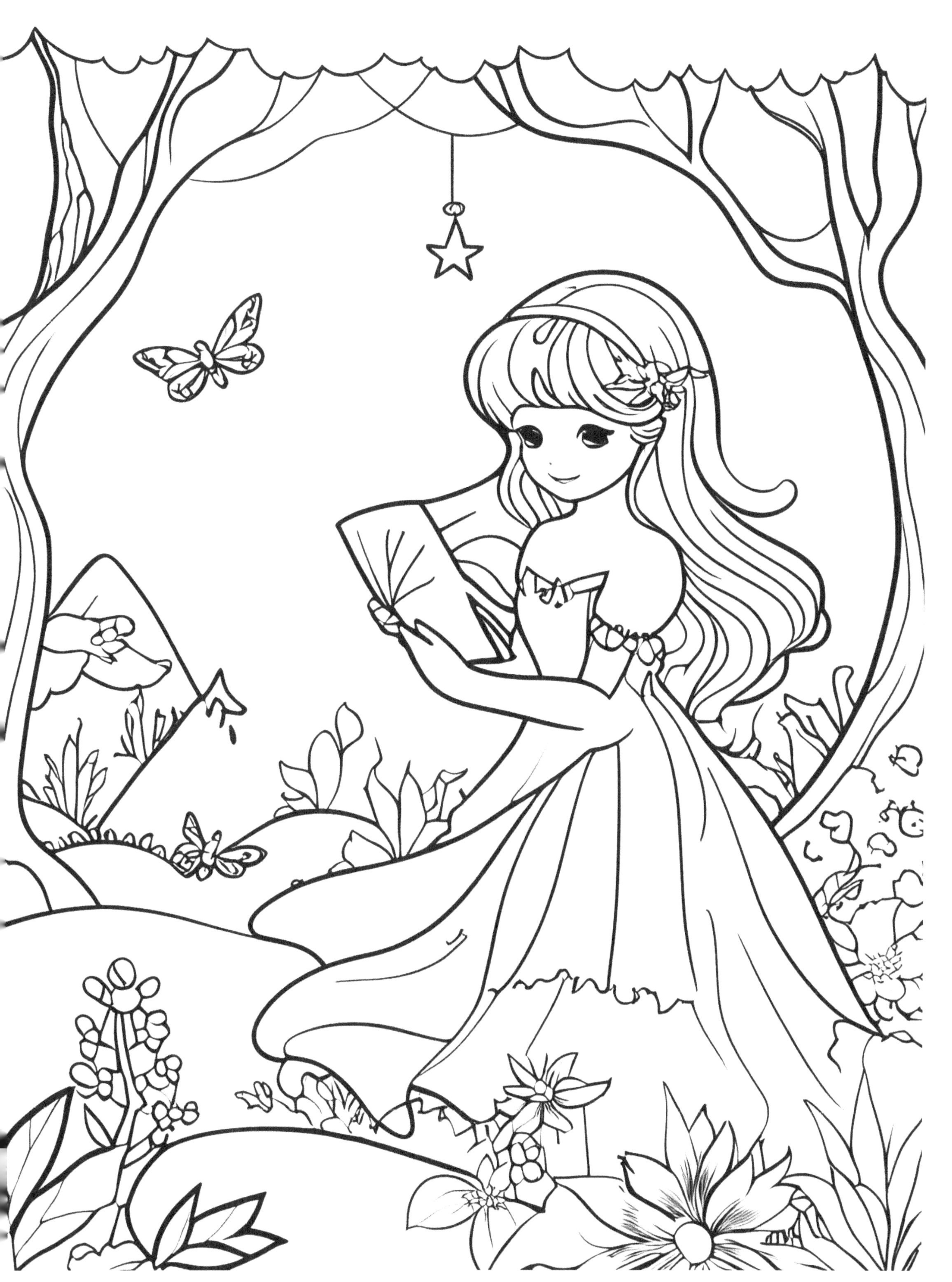

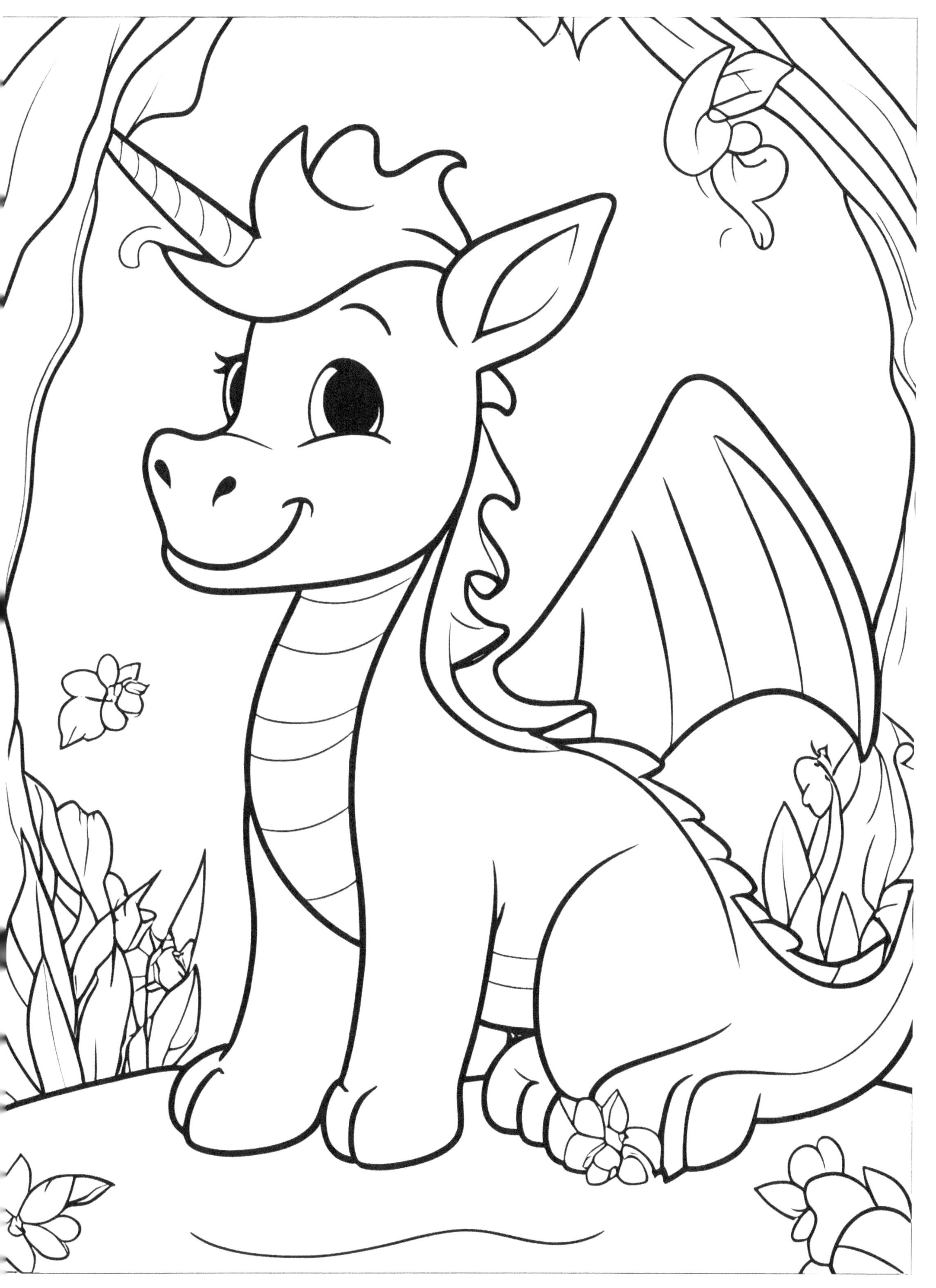

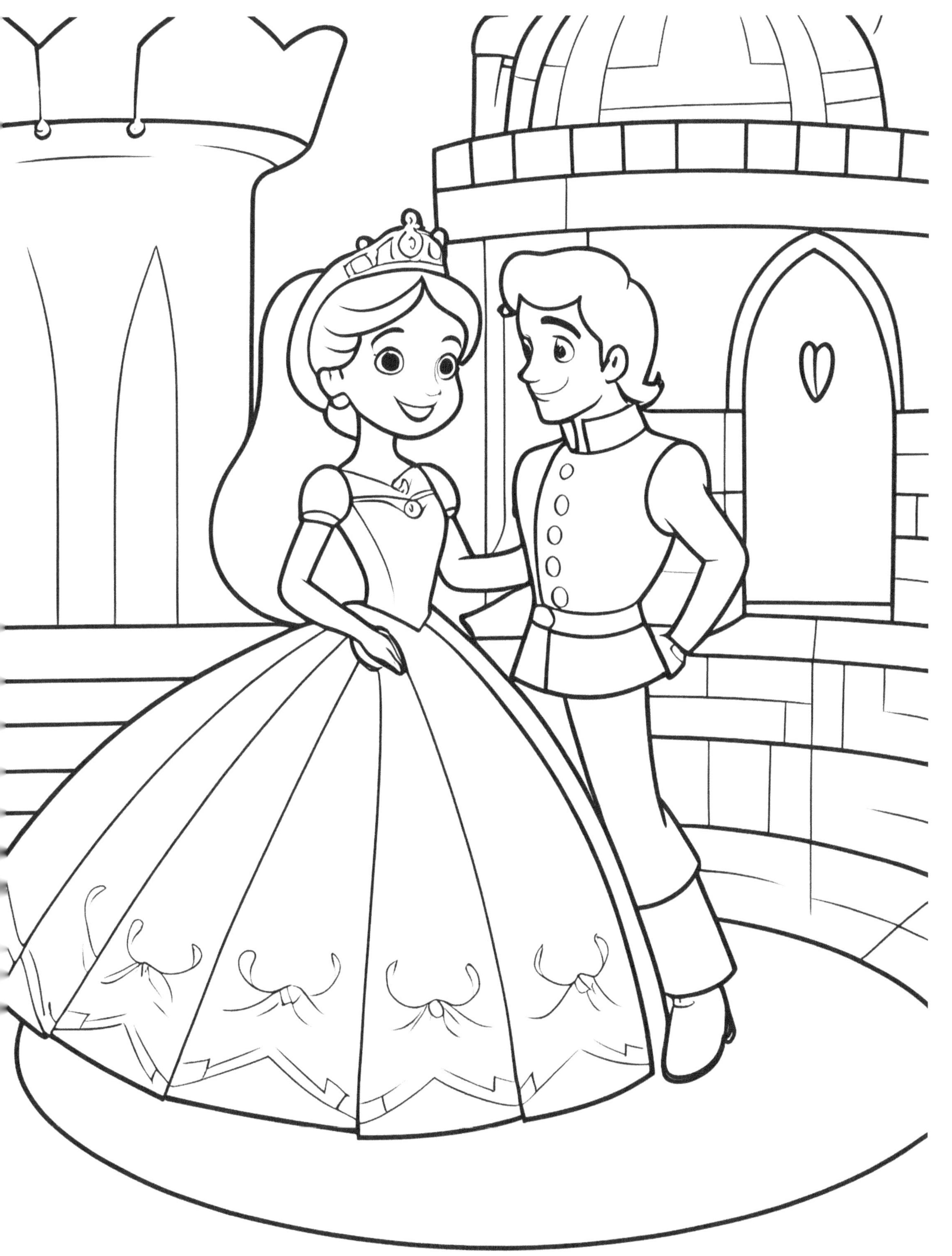

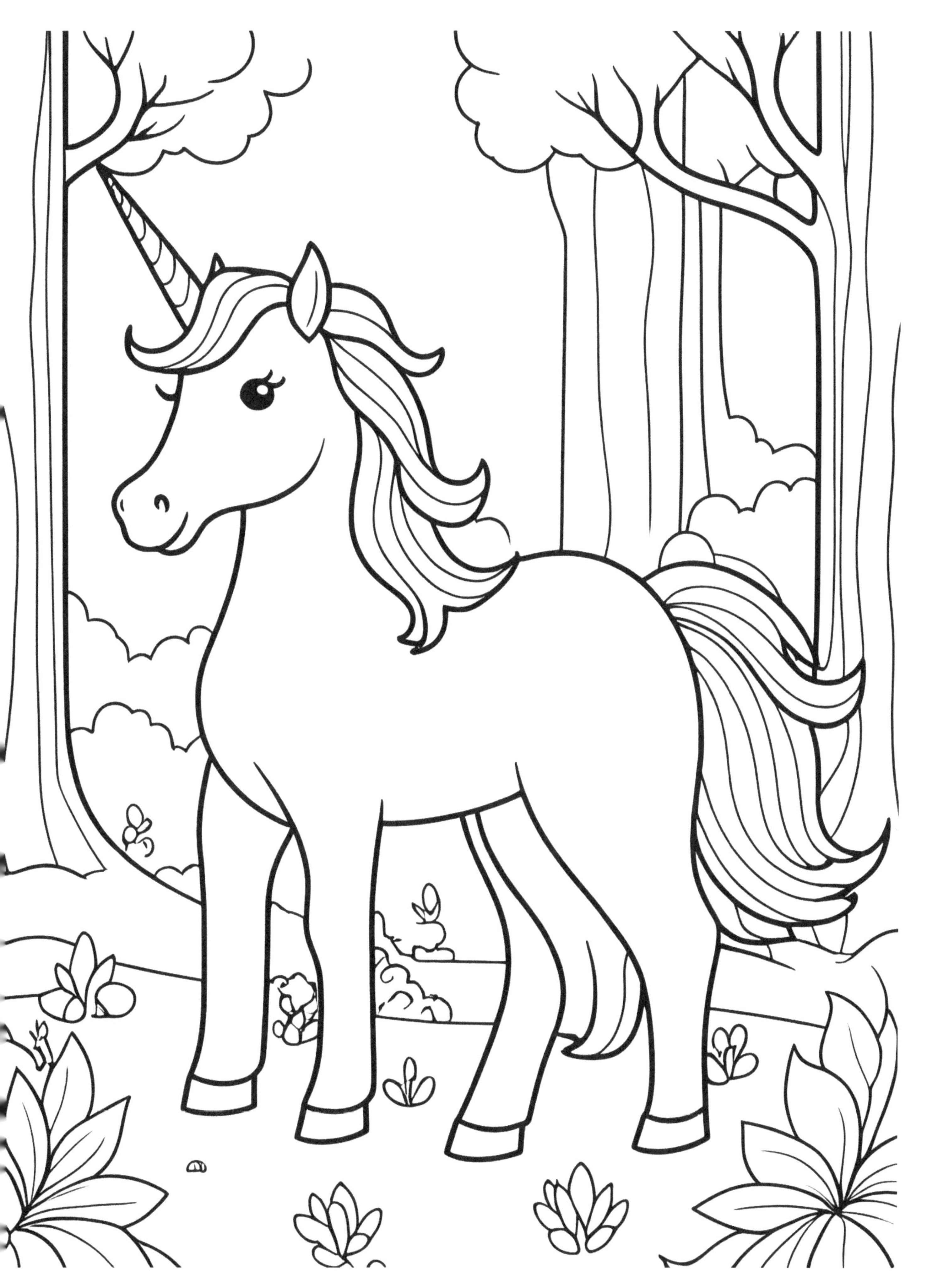

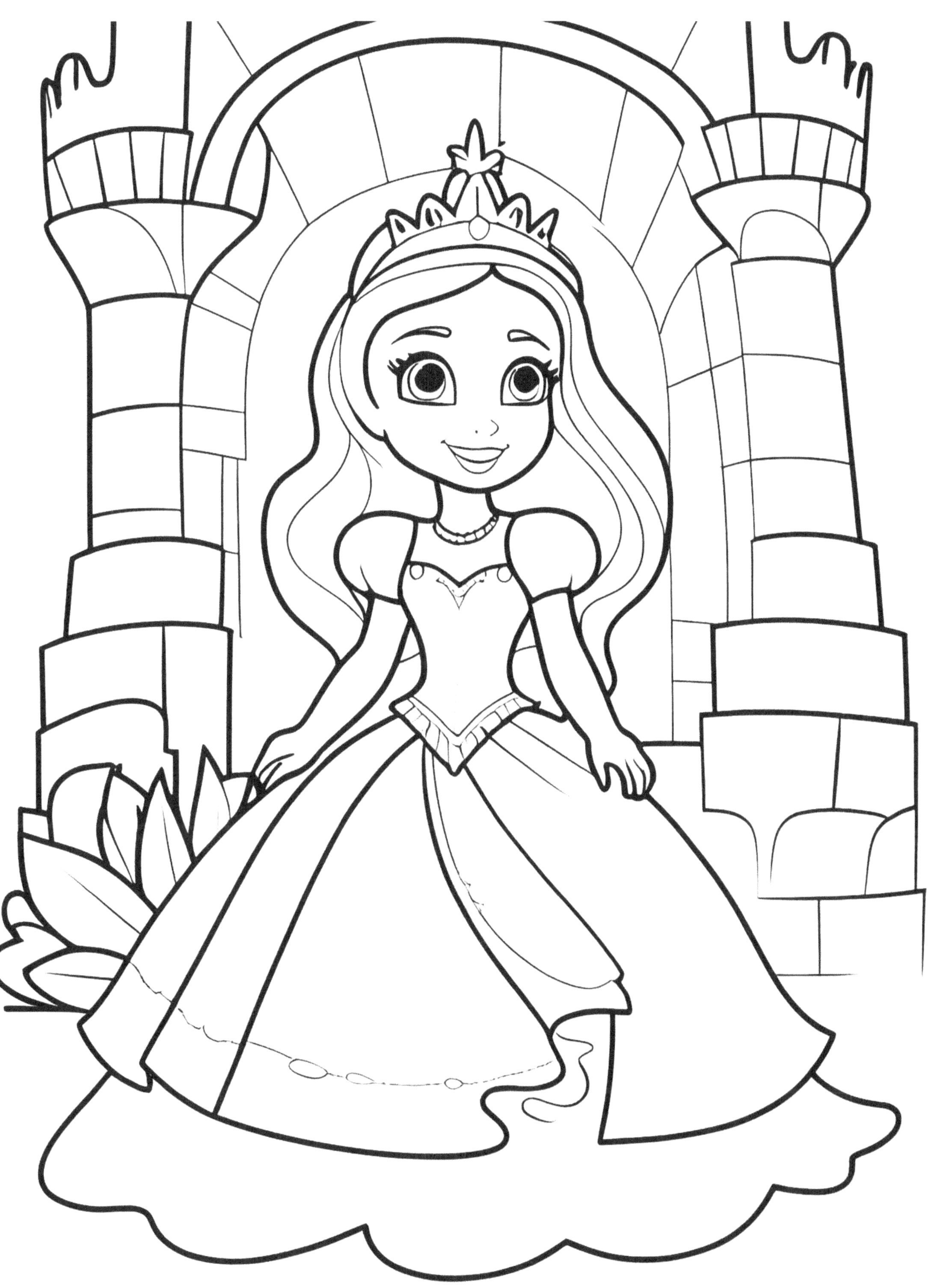

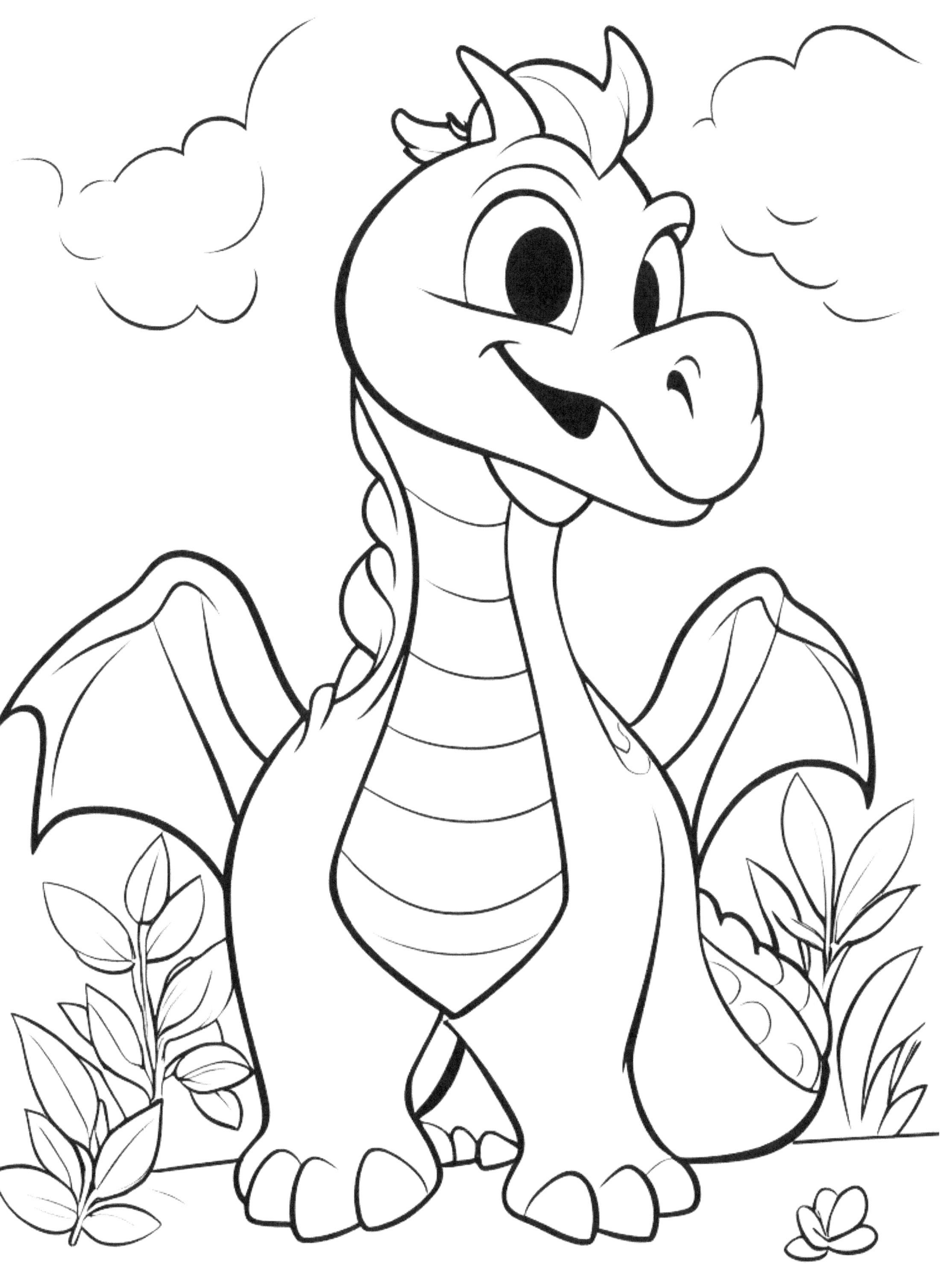

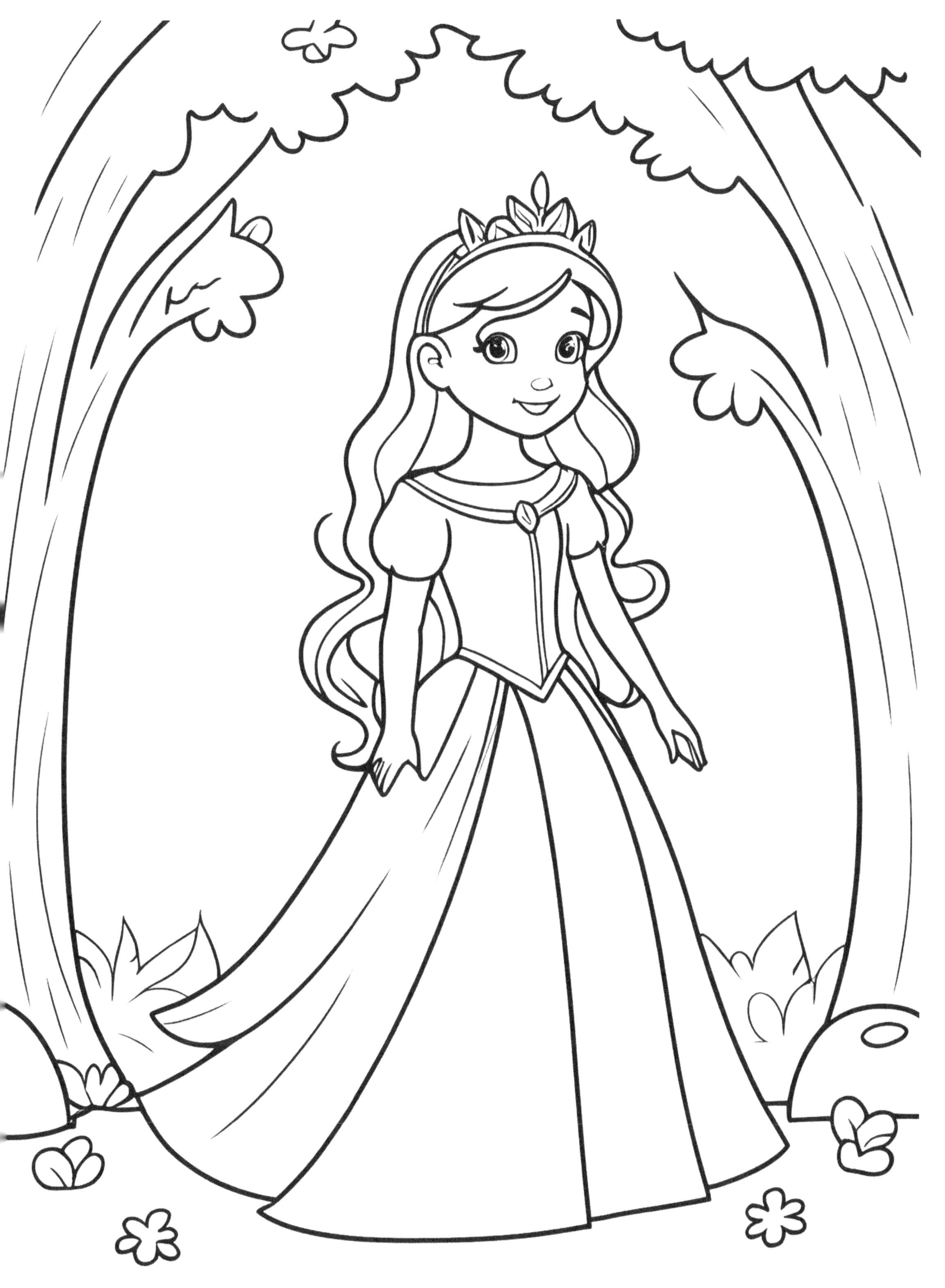

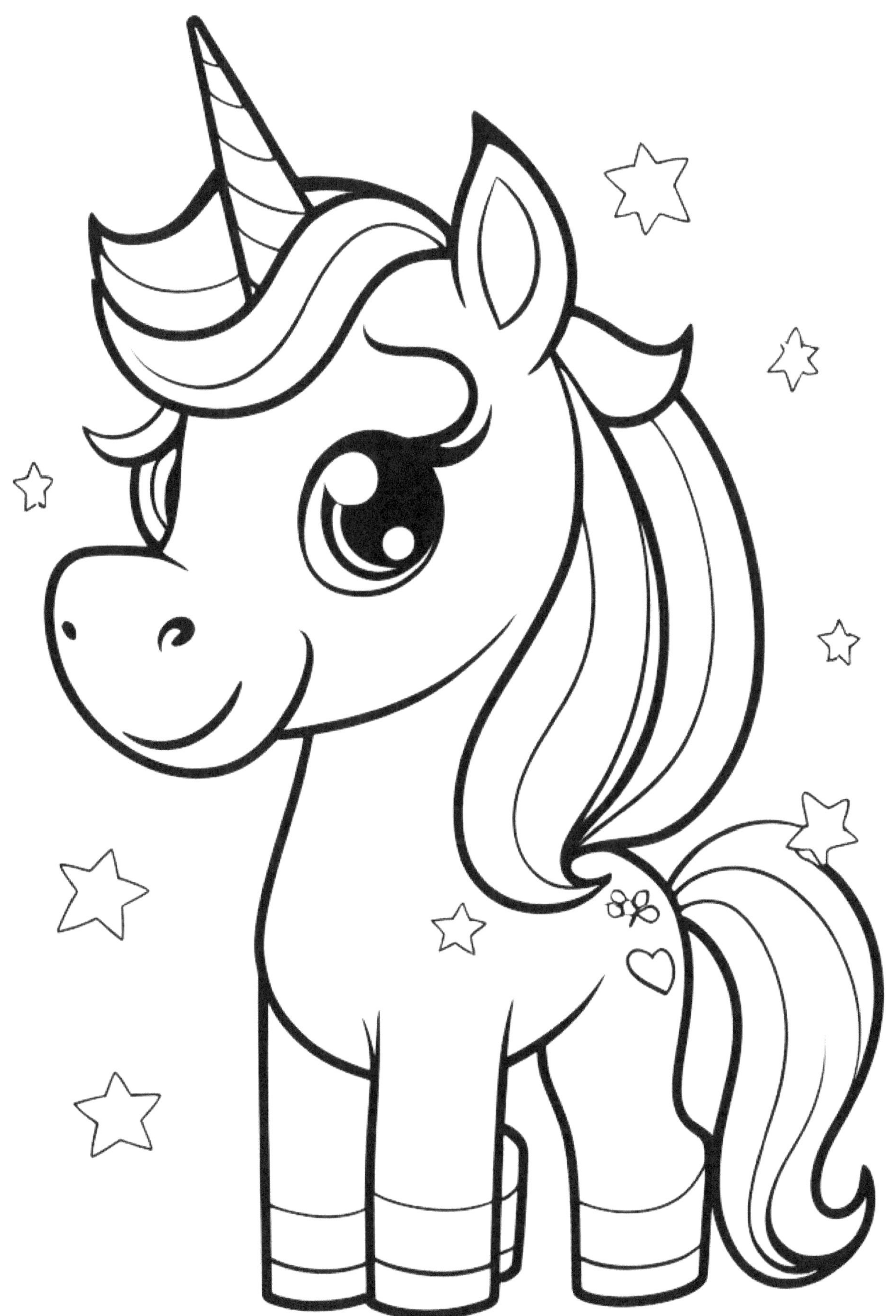

www.ingramcontent.com/pod-product-compliance
Lightning Source LLC
Chambersburg PA
CBHW080040260726
48658CB00007B/2683